Prayer Book
for
Earnest
Christians

Containing fine prayers,
rich in spirit,
with which devout Christian hearts
may take comfort
in every season
and in every need

O come, let us worship and bow down,
let us kneel before the Lord, our Maker!
　Psalm 95:6

But the hour is coming, and is now here,
when the true worshipers
will worship the Father in spirit and truth,
for the Father seeks such as these to worship him.
　John 4:23

Pray in the Spirit at all times
in every prayer and supplication.
To that end keep alert
and always persevere in supplication
for all the saints.
　Ephesians 6:18

I will pray with the spirit,
but I will pray with the mind also.
　1 Corinthians 14:15

Prayer Book

for

Earnest Christians

Die ernsthafte Christenpflicht

Translated and edited
by Leonard Gross

HERALD PRESS
Scottdale, Pennsylvania
Waterloo, Ontario

Library of Congress Cataloging-in-Publication Data
Ernsthafte Christenpflicht, Die. English
    Prayer book for earnest Christians / translated and edited by
Leonard Gross.
    Includes bibliographical references.
    ISBN 0-8361-9044-0
    1. Prayers. I. Gross, Leonard.
BV260.E7613 1996
242'.8097—dc20   96-8616

The paper used in this publication is recycled and meets the mini-
mum requirements of American National Standard for Information
Sciences—Permanence of Paper for Printed Library Materials, ANSI
Z39.48-1984.

✠

Contents

Die
Ernsthaffte
Christen-Pflicht/
Darinnen
Schöne Geistreiche
Gebetter/

Darmit
Sich fromme Christen-Hertzen zu allen Zeiten und in allen Nöhten trösten können

Nebst einem Anhang
Einer
Aus dem blutigen Schau-Spiel übersetzter Geschichte zweyer Blut-Zeugen der Warheit, Hans von Ober dam u. Valerius des Schulmeisters.

Gedruckt in Ephrata
im Jahr 1 7 4 5.

Foreword

The language of fervent prayer comes through clearly in this new translation of *Die ernsthafte Christenpflicht*. These prayers were offered three centuries ago by devout Christians in Europe and much used by Anabaptists. Amish and Mennonites carried them in their trunks and in their hearts when they crossed the ocean to the New World. Their voices of prayer span the barriers of time, language, and culture, and are as fitting today as then.

These heartfelt prayers express thanks for God's caring protection, sincere confession, longing for God's merciful forgiveness of sin, and gratefulness for God's grace, which crowns the daily sunrise. Prayers for evening, morning, and special occasions reflect a desire for lives of obedience, hearts full of peace, and congregations of love and harmony. Pastoral concerns appear in prayers for the depressed, the poor, the weak, the sick, and the mentally handicapped; for widows and orphans; for persecutors and the persecuted.

Fifty years ago, Edward Yoder was using this classic devotional book and noted in his journal that it was "truly inspirational and deeply spiritual in tone and thought." He lamented that his generation of Mennonites, adopting English, had "cut themselves off so completely . . . from the rich treasures of their heritage."

Now these treasures have been reclaimed. Like the Psalms, these enduring prayers provide a language of devotion and commitment that will enrich personal, family, and congregational worship. They truly are "rich in spirit" and give comfort to "devout Christian hearts . . . in every season and in every need." We commend them to you for regular use.

Readers may want to choose appropriate portions of long prayers for use in public worship. Pastors will find many concerns and themes that can be readily adapted for pastoral prayers. Personal pronouns can be adjusted for either personal or corporate worship.

These prayers will also make a contribution to the literature of spiritual direction and spiritual retreats, whether personal or guided. Much of the literature of spirituality, while relevant and useful, has been borrowed from other theological traditions. Here is a wellspring of fervent spiritual expression from the Mennonite and Amish experience of earlier centuries.

The Historical Committee of the Mennonite Church recognized this need when it took action to sponsor the translation of this historic book of prayers. The committee sensed the growing thirst for a deep spirituality, the renewal of interest in the church's heritage, and the constant need for clear identity and vision.

We hope that through these prayers God will "shape the ordering of our lives," "encourage the work of our hands," and "graciously equip us with true faith, good hope, and genuine Christian love."

—John E. Sharp, Director
  Historical Committee of the Mennonite Church

Preface

One of the best-kept publishing secrets within the Anabaptist tradition is the existence of a small tome, *Die ernsthafte Christenpflicht*.[1] The first known edition was in 1708, and it is still in print. Among Amish and Mennonite books, this has the most (65) known North American printings, plus six printings of selections in English. Worldwide, its 88 known complete editions or reprints (counting this one) is superseded only by *The Wandering Soul* with its 127 known printings.

Now for the first time, all the prayers of the current edition of the *Christenpflicht* are available in English translation—including the seven prayers appended in the 1992 edition from an older source.

In 1991 the Mennonite Publishing House (Herald Press) printed its last edition of the German *Christenpflicht*. In 1992 Pathway Publishers of Aylmer, Ontario, issued a new edition, expanded by adding an appendix of additional prayers, as suggested by its senior editor, Joseph Stoll. These seven prayers, not found in the American edition, were taken from the first (1846) Canadian edition of the *Christenpflicht*.[2]

The prayers translated here thus include all the prayers in the most recent American edition, plus selected prayers from the Canadian edition. All together, these are the prayers in the current Pathway Publishers' edition of the *Christenpflicht.*[3]

Page numbers of the 1992 German edition are enclosed in brackets: [4], [5], and so on. In this translation, many sentences and paragraphs have been divided for easier reading, while giving full respect to the sense of the original. Modern speech tends to be terse; here the style of linked synonyms has been preserved. Punctuation has been fitted to the translation, but the exclamation mark following direct address has been preserved even in midsentence.

The prayers are saturated with scriptural quotations, terms, and allusions, based on Luther's *Bibel.* Many of the quotations are slightly adapted to the context of the prayer. Quotation marks are not included in the original nor here. The superscript reference numbers will guide the reader to notes in the back of the book which identify some but not nearly all of the quotations and allusions.

I wish to recognize and thank Angela Showalter for copyediting the main body of prayers, Suzanne Gross for copyediting the prayers in the appendix, and Marilyn Voran for proofreading for style. S. David Garber, Herald Press editor, deserves special recognition for his editorial suggestions throughout, based on careful comparison with the original German. Garber supplied most of the biblical references in the notes, none of which are in the original German edition. Thanks also to John E. Sharp, who read the translation for style and prepared the index.

—*Leonard Gross, Translator and Editor*
  Historical Committee of the Mennonite Church
  Goshen, Indiana

Prayer Book
for
Earnest
Christians

✠

A Fine Morning Prayer

O Lord, almighty God and heavenly Father, you have created us as human beings, formed us and given us life.[4] You placed us into this world to obtain our sustenance with grief and toil until we again return to the earth, from which we were taken. You have also set for us a time for our life, that we may fear and love you, and hold fast to you wholeheartedly.

Just as you have given us the day for work, so also have you, through your divine kindness, ordained the night for rest. This rest we have enjoyed, merciful God and Father! under your gracious fatherly shelter and keeping. For this it is fitting that we praise, honor, and glorify you from the bottom of our hearts and the depths of our souls. [4]

O almighty God and heavenly Father! forgive us for whatever we did last night or on any day of our lives that was not time spent in a holy way, whether through misuse of your blessings, transgression of your holy commands, or neglect of our duties in words, actions, and thoughts, while asleep or awake. However we may have sinned against you, we confess with remorse and sorrow that such has happened. May you in mercy forgive us and pardon our sin, O heavenly Father! through the shed blood of Jesus Christ, your dear Son.

O heavenly Father! you have again let this day dawn. Help us remember that it is your gracious gift. Teach us to understand gratefully why you are again bestowing this glorious gift. As a merciful Father, you let your beautiful sun rise above our heads. Thus may we spend all the days of our lives following your will, preparing ourselves for the eternally long and everlasting day that you will create through your grace.

Holy Father! grant that we may understand and learn to forsake the night of darkness and sin, and be freed from it. May we walk in the clear light of your [5] divine grace. Help us lay aside the works of darkness and put on the armor of light, so we may walk honorably as in the day.

O merciful God, let us radiate the light of your divine mercy. May we constantly keep you, O God and Father! foremost before our eyes in all we do or leave undone. You see everything, right now, with your eyes like a flame of fire,[5] even what we are thinking and planning. And we know that you do not leave a good deed unrewarded nor an evil deed unpunished. Therefore, give us grace that we may spend all our days in a way that will bring praise to your holy name.

We pray, O holy Father! that just as you have loved us, we may be obedient to you with childlike love. Just as we are experiencing your fatherly love, may we in turn love our neighbor as ourselves. May we do nothing contrary to this love, so we may truly deal justly with our neighbor.

Holy Father! we pray that we may also enjoy with moderation all the gifts you have supplied for our needs, using them solely for their intended purpose. May we not misuse them through extravagance, [6] greed, or selfish pleasures. Give us hearts willing to share, which do not complain about food and drink, or worry about physical nourishment. Teach us instead to place our trust in you and to await your divine help and grace. Give us a broken, lowly, and contrite spirit, a penitent heart and true gentleness, and a genuine hunger and thirst for your righteousness.

Give us today a heart that is pure in your sight, O God! that we may see you. God of love and peace! grant us your eternal peace and grace that we may at all times show ourselves to be peace-loving in our relations with one another, avoiding all evil strife and dispute. And help us, with gentle spirit and quiet heart, to bear patiently all the calamities we may encounter in this life—whether the cross, or grief, or disgrace, or other misfortune.

O Lord! since you are our God and Creator, direct our life and walk according to your holy and divine will. All our works and deeds are in your hands. We commit ourselves into your hands, O holy Father! with body and soul and all that we have. Rule over us, [7] and advance the work of our hands, O God! according to your divine will.

We also pray for all people, everywhere, especially for our fellow believers wherever they may be scattered on the face of the earth. We pray as well for all troubled and desperate hearts, suffering and in need. And we pray for our persecutors, for they know not what they are doing.

We also pray for all the ministers of your church, for all rulers and authorities, and for all others for whom we ought to pray. . . .[6]

O Lord! let all of them together enjoy and partake of your mercy and your comfort. We ask this, O holy Father! in the name of your dear Son, Jesus Christ, who promised us that you would respond favorably when we call upon you in his name, praying with reverent and believing hearts: Our Father . . . [the Lord's Prayer; see page 21].

O Lord! may your gracious eyes be open upon us day and night. Take us into your divine care and protection. Judge, guide, and bless all our undertakings and works, to your honor. Amen. [8]

⳩

A Fine Evening Prayer
For Daily Use

O Lord God! dear merciful heavenly Father, you have for our illumination so kindly let the light of heaven shine upon us.[7] You have also granted us this fleeting day to be used according to your holy will, to be lived out in godly devotion.

For these gracious gifts of yours, O holy Father! we give you praise and thanks, honor and eternal glory. We pray, dear gracious Father! forgive us what we have sinned against you this day acting against your divine will. In repentance and sorrow we confess our sins, that through idleness and lack of concern we have grievously sinned against you.

O holy Father! forgive us for the sake of your beloved Son, Jesus Christ, in whose name we now pray. Accept us through him into your divine reconciliation. Through your Child, [Jesus Christ,] may we have true peace with you, O Holy Father! and keep that peace forever.

We pray, O holy Father! that now in this coming night, which you [9] have ordained for our rest, and in the whole time of our life, we may remain under your divine care and protection. Shield us against all the powers of darkness and the treachery of the deceitful enemy, who without ceasing prowls around us day and night, to ruin our souls. O holy Father! protect and preserve us from his treachery and temptation, and cover us with your wings of mercy.

Holy Father! let our bodies rest peacefully, without stain of body or soul, according to your holy and divine

will. Likewise, let our hearts, our spirits, and our thoughts
remain awake in you forever, looking forward to the coming of your dear Son. May we prepare ourselves in conformity with your divine counsel and await your glorious
coming with joy.

Holy and merciful Father! we pray that the light of
your divine grace may shine upon us. May we not be
overcome by the night of darkness in which the whole
world lies, nor fall asleep unto death. Instead, may we
pass through death into life. Let this all be to the praise,
honor, and glory of your holy, excellent, and majestic [10]
name, and to our eternal salvation.

O holy Father! let us enjoy and be partakers of all this
in the name of your beloved Son, Jesus Christ. We also
pray, dear God and Father! for all the needs facing your
dear children: for those who are weak, troubled, and
depressed; for those suffering on account of your holy
Word and name; and also for those who persecute us, for
they know not what they are doing.[8] O Lord! send loyal
workers into your harvest, that they may proclaim to us
your holy Word according to your will.[9]

We pray as well for the authorities and rulers of
nations and cities, and for everyone with a worried, anxious, or hopeless heart.

O holy Father! you know all their needs and also our
needs. Open your gracious eyes upon them and upon all
of us, graciously supporting us with your strength. Let us
your creatures not perish but be received and kept unto
eternal salvation.

We ask all this, O holy Father! in the name of your
dear Son, Jesus Christ, [11] our Lord and Savior, who has

taught us to pray in his name and say, Our Father . . . [the
Lord's Prayer].

O holy Father! all of us together commit ourselves into
your hands. Protect us as a body, O God. Surround us
with your holy angels, and lead us with your holy and
good Spirit through this vale of tears, until our blessed
end[10] and we are joyfully raised up and received into
heaven. This we pray, holy Father! through your dearly
beloved Son, Jesus Christ. Amen.

✠

A Fine General Prayer
for Many Occasions and Times of Need
For Daily Use

O Lord, almighty God, holy and heavenly Father, you
alone are eternal and all-powerful, living and reigning
from everlasting to everlasting.[11] You are the one before
whom we come and appear, bending the knees of our
heart.[12] You are the one to whom we pray: may you have
mercy upon us. Cleanse our mouths, tongues, and lips,
and especially our hands and hearts. May we become worthy of calling upon your holy name, which is great, and
to praise and give [12] thanks.

We confess that you are an almighty, abundantly sufficient God, full of all that is good. There is no other god,
either in heaven or on earth, that is your equal. We know
that you are a good, gracious, and merciful God.
Therefore, with one mind we want to call and petition
you, as your dear Child, Jesus Christ, has taught. Make us
fit and able to speak, and to say in spirit and in truth:

Our Father who art in heaven,
Hallowed be thy name.
Thy kingdom come.
Thy will be done on earth,
      as it is in heaven.
Give us this day our daily bread.
And forgive us our debts,
      as we forgive our debtors.
And lead us not into temptation,
      but deliver us from evil.
For thine is the kingdom and the power
      and the glory, forever. Amen.[13]

O holy Father in heaven! we must praise and exalt you far above all other things and creatures, for you are our God and Creator. You have formed us, made us after your image, and endowed us with many more gifts than all other creatures.

While we were dead in our sins and were your enemies, [13] you had mercy upon us and did not spare your only begotten Son, but offered him up for us all in the most despised death on the cross. There he shed his innocent blood for us, died for our sins to justify us, arose from the dead, and ascended to heaven.[14] He preached and proclaimed a holy, eternal gospel, intending it for us. Thus he called us to your blessed communion and made us heirs of your eternal heavenly kingdom.

Therefore, we acknowledge that above all other creatures we are obliged to praise and thank you, to glorify and honor you, O holy Father! Because of this we are bowing before you on our knees. But, holy God and

Father! we are not fully capable or worthy to thank your holy name as much as you deserve. For we have so often sinned before you with words and deeds, even with our vain and empty life and walk. Yet we come before you and confess our sins, praying in the name of our Lord Jesus, your dear Son, that you may still decide to show us mercy.

Have mercy upon [14] us, and do not judge or treat us according to our deeds and merits, but according to your great compassion. Blot out all our transgressions, and graciously accept us once again. Yes, holy Father, clothe us with the true genuine faith, with steadfastness and truth, and with the knowledge of your holy Word and Spirit.

May you, holy Father, always be our path and guide, our refuge and haven, our comfort and strength. Set our feet, mind, heart, and spirit on the way to your divine peace. Cause your holy and divine Word, which you allow us to hear, to be living and active in our hearts, so we may please you and serve you till the end of our life.

O holy Father! we pray for all our dear fellow members, for brothers and sisters, wherever they are scattered under the heavens and on the earth, whether far away or near us, on water or on land. All their names are well known to you. O Lord! surround them with your holy angels, for your eyes look upon those who fear you.

Grant all of them, along with us, obedient hearts, full of faith, wisdom, and understanding, so we will know how we are to live, walk, and please you. [15] Fill our hearts as well with love, peace, and true brotherly unity. For your love is the true bond, with which you hold your chosen ones together under your care and protection, through your divine grace and invincible strength.[15]

O holy Father, we pray for all those who have left the way of truth out of weakness, or through anxiety and desperation, cross and tribulation, or unbelief, yet who now once more desire your grace and the petition of your faithful people. O Lord! show your steadfast mercy to them. Grant them true regret and repentance for their mistakes and offenses. Graciously accept them again as your children.

You have created so many thousands of people, and so few acknowledge and fear you. Instead, they are being held back through false teachers and deceitful workers. Therefore, O holy Father! protect us from false doctrine, false faith, false love, and evil reason. Above all, shield us from that which might confuse us, hinder us, or separate us from your love and righteousness.

O holy Father in heaven! we pray that you might consider how great your harvest is, and yet how few are the true workers. May you yet awaken and send holy and [16] faithful servants[16] into your harvest. Send those who have found grace before your holy eyes, who may proclaim to us your holy Word without pride, deception, or hypocrisy. May they seek nothing but your praise, your honor, and your glory, and the salvation of souls. Send those who are preparing an obedient people for you, zealous and equipped for every good work; those who might gather your people in love, peace, and unity, though now they are still divided by a great lack of understanding.[17]

O holy Father in heaven, we ask you to take away all our ignorance. If there is anything in us displeasing to you and yet hidden from our awareness, grant that we may recognize it. Move our hearts to forsake it willingly. If we still do not know what is pleasing to you, and it is concealed from us, grant that we may recognize it. Give us an obedient heart to accept it gladly, so all we do or leave undone will be well-pleasing to you.

O holy Father in heaven, we pray for all who are suffering for the sake of your Word and witness: those in prison and in chains; those exiled, banished, despised, suppressed, and robbed of their possessions; those deprived of all human consolation. O Lord! even so, console them with [17] your divine comfort.

Ease their suffering, and grant them, alongside all their hard trials and tribulations, a gracious conclusion and steadfastness, according to your boundless goodness and mercy. May they, fixed and firm, stand for your name and confess your Child, Jesus, before all people, so he in turn may confess them before you.

O holy Father in heaven! be merciful to all who hate, slander, disdain, and persecute you and us, and yet do not know what they are doing. Do not hold them guilty on our account. But help them recognize how seriously they are sinning against you, so they may become alarmed, make amends, and repent.

O holy Father in heaven! we ask you to shatter and destroy the decrees and charges of all our enemies by which they strike against us. Save us, just as from the beginning of the world you have saved all those who placed their inner faith and trust in you.

May you also, O holy Father! show us mercy, just as a compassionate father shows mercy to his children. Send down your holy angels from the heights of heaven, to go ahead of us and fight against our enemies and adversaries. May they save us from the hand of those who hate us, until [18] the time when you, O Lord! acknowledge us to be virtuous and able to endure everything that you have commanded, without retreating from your Word, to the right or to the left.

May we be found to be true witnesses of your holy Word, so our names will be found in the book of eternal life.[18] May we through your grace be worthy of escaping the coming evil and your fierce wrath, and be joyous in appearing before your holy face. May you choose to be a gracious judge over us, O Lord Jesus Christ! so we, along with your chosen children, may rejoice in your everlasting kingdom, to the praise and glory of your holy name, always and forever.

O holy Father in heaven! we pray for every king and ruler, and especially for those under whose care and protection we live. O Lord, help them to understand why they were created, made, and ordained by you, that they may do and carry out your divine will. Implant your fear into their hearts, so they do not misuse the power which you have given them, but use it rather to protect and care for the devout, to instill fear, and to punish evildoers and the unrighteous.

Moreover, give [19] them wisdom and understanding to govern their countries, peoples, and cities so we may lead a quiet and godly life under their rule, O Lord! according to your holy and divine pleasure. And as much as we now through your divine grace are enjoying this kind of life, we give you deserved praise and thanks. O Lord! grant that we may use this freedom with deep gratitude.

O holy Father in heaven, we pray for all the widows and orphans; all those aged and infirm, and the senile; for all the sick, the forsaken, and the desolate; for those in hunger and need, in mental distress, despair, and discouragement. O Lord! you know them all well. Console them with your divine comfort. Teach them to bear patiently your fatherly chastisement and to await your gracious help as they depart from this life.

O holy Father in heaven, we pray for all those true-hearted people[19] round about, who love us and treat us well, who show compassion by sharing their food and drink, home and shelter. O Lord! reward them richly with favor. Since they gladly listen to your Word but do not have the strength to commit themselves to you in obedience, grant them the needed strength through your Holy Spirit to receive your [20] Word, and let it be planted in them with meekness, that it may save their souls.

O holy Father! we pray that you would protect us from warfare and bloodshed in our land. Guard and shield us from unkind people who dispute your holy Word and truth.

Take away from us as well all the sin that clings to us and oppresses us, such as anger, hostility, envy, hate, impurity, pride, and greed, the root of all evil.[20] Also take from us a malicious heart, with all unrighteousness, and create in us a pure heart. Renew in us an honest and willing spirit. Teach us your ways, O Lord! and grant us grace so we may walk therein till the end of our life.

O holy Father in heaven! we give you praise and thanks, honor and everlasting glory, that you have shown mercy to us and given us food and drink, clothes and homes, bedding and nourishment—for soul and body. For all good gifts come from you alone, O Lord. Grant that we may use them in accord with your holy will. [21]

Now into your hands we commit ourselves, all of us together, children and adults, young and old, body and soul, and all that belongs to us. O Lord! be concerned for our lives. Raise us up, and transplant us from sin into righteousness. Make us worthy and able to do your holy and divine will.

O holy Father! together we ask you this, in the name of your dear Son, Jesus Christ, through the strength and help of the Holy Spirit. May you be forever praised, adored, and glorified from now till eternity. Amen, Amen.

⳨

Another Fine Prayer

O almighty God and heavenly Father! we pray to you, the One who knows and recognizes all our flaws and pettiness. Without your help and grace we would not exist or be able to do anything. So we ask you, holy Father, to grant us grace that together we may call to you, praying and making our petitions in spirit and in truth. May this, O Lord! serve to your praise, honor, and glory, bringing [22] comfort to us who are gathered, and salvation, and eternal life. Amen.

Thus may we always be able to pray with upright hearts, Our Father . . . [the Lord's Prayer].

O Lord! almighty God and heavenly Father, we ask you to clothe us with faith, love, loyalty, and truth, and with the knowledge of your holy Word and Spirit. Be our constant path and guide, our refuge and haven. Set our feet, mind, heart, and soul upon the path of your divine peace, that we may serve you as your dear children until our end.

We ask you, holy Father, to have mercy upon us now in these last and dangerous times. Pardon and forgive us for everything in which we have sinned and acted against you, whether this happened with or without our awareness, in word or deed, in intention or thought. O Lord! be gracious and merciful to us. Enliven and strengthen in our hearts your holy Word, which you have allowed us to hear. May it increase and thrive among us, that you, O Lord! may find growth among us, so we may serve you as your obedient children until our end.

We pray to you, holy Father! for all [23] our fellow members throughout the whole wide world, our beloved brothers and sisters. Whether they are scattered or gathered, suffering cross and distress, in bonds and prison for your holy name's sake, or perhaps with serious illness—strengthen and comfort them with your grace. Let them not swerve to the right or to the left. Keep them in your holy Word and truth until the end of their lives. Give them grace and endurance, that they may serve your Word with patience.

Do not let us, your children, be tempted beyond our strength, but make a path for us, and show us the way past temptation and trouble. Grant that we may be able to bear and endure it. This we ask, holy Father, in the name of your dear Son, our Lord and Savior, Jesus Christ.

We pray, holy Father, grant us mercy and draw us

together under your care and protection. May no discord or division come among us (if this petition is not against your divine will). But protect us, O Lord! against false faith and evil reason, and above all, against whatever might lead us astray or separate us from your love and righteousness.

[24] We ask you, O Lord of the harvest! to consider that your harvest is so great, and yet the loyal workers are few. So raise up for us, O Lord! faithful shepherds and workers in your harvest, servants[21] after your own heart who have found grace before your eyes to proclaim your holy Word and righteousness. May they preach without pride, deception, or hypocrisy, so that through the praise of many persons your holy name may be honored and glorified.

Make for your holy Word a path and a way for us and for all who desire from their hearts to be converted, and for all who hunger and thirst for your love and righteousness. May these all be assured and taught, fed and given drink.

We pray, holy Father! for all your messengers and servants whom you have sent out to proclaim and preach your holy Word and righteousness. Through your Holy Spirit give them words and wisdom, intelligence and understanding, to proclaim your holy Word and righteousness according to your holy and divine will, and according to our deficiency and need.

We pray, holy Father! for all people in the whole wide world about whom it is possible to pray. [25] We also pray for kings and all authorities, especially for those under whom your people are living. Keep them from stretching out their hands over your people to shed innocent blood. Instead, cause them to act and reign as you have determined and ordained, to punish the evil and to protect and care for the good. Thus may we and all who fear your name lead a quiet and peaceful life here on earth.

We pray, holy Father! for all our enemies, who insult, hate, slander, and persecute us for the sake of your holy name. Do not hold it against them for our sakes, since they do not know what they are doing. Instead, dash to pieces their harsh measures and assaults by which they strike out against your Word and righteousness. If it is not asking against your divine will, call them to repentance, that they might turn from their failure and sin.

We pray to you, heavenly Father! for all truehearted people who desire your grace and our petitions, and also for all who are weak, mentally handicapped, distraught, and depressed. Be gracious and merciful to them. Pardon and forgive them for any sins they have committed against you, whether this happened with [26] or without their awareness. Increase and strengthen their faith, hope, and love, that they may be accepted into your holy covenant.

We pray, heavenly Father! for all truehearted people who have shown us compassion and proved it with food and drink, with home and refuge. For your holy name's sake, repay them with blessing, and fill their needs and wants, both in body and in soul.

We pray, heavenly Father! for all who have been driven away and pushed aside from your love and righteousness, those who have wandered away from your truth, through anxiety and trouble, and through cross and distress. Or perhaps they were caught as in a landslide and have fallen down and again desire your grace and our prayers. So we pray, heavenly Father! give them strength once more to show remorse and to repent of their failure and sin. Graciously accept them again as your children, all who fear you from the heart.

We praise and thank you, heavenly Father! for creating all things, heaven and earth, the sea and everything on it and in it, and for keeping faith forever.[22] We thank you for bringing justice to the one who [27] suffers injustice, and for all whom you have saved, who have believed and placed their trust in you from the beginning of the world, and who have remained in your fear. May you indeed continue to save them.

Give us also a steadfast, living faith and a firm trust, a holy hope and a genuine love. May we in this manner serve you and keep your commandments wholeheartedly, with joyful souls and with all our strength, to the end, whether unto life or unto death.

We ask you, holy Father! to grant us your mercy just as a compassionate father shows his children mercy. Send your holy angel from above as our guide, to go before us and fight against our enemies and opponents, and to save us from the hand of all those who hate you. So protect us until the time when you acknowledge us to be virtuous and able to suffer and endure whatever you have determined for us. Thus may we not retreat from your holy Word, either to the right or to the left. This we pray, O holy Father! in the name of Jesus Christ. Amen.

Almighty God and heavenly Father! we offer you praise and thanksgiving [28] for all your fatherly grace and mercy which you are giving and showing us now, in these last and dangerous times. Consider now our great weakness, and lead us at all times in your name. Draw us together under your powerful divine hand, your fatherly care and protection, and your divine grace and power, which cannot be conquered.

Care for us gathered here, and give us obedient hearts to do your will. Thus may we be worthy to escape all [the danger] that will come to pass, and may we together rejoice in your eternal kingdom. We pray, O holy Father! prepare for us constantly a path and a way, a place and a home, and friends and a guide, so we may live and walk safely in the presence of all our enemies.

We pray, O merciful Father! for all who are anxious, weak, sick, mentally handicapped, and depressed; for widows and orphans; for the aged and the evil-minded; and for those who have lost their reasoning powers. With your grace, strengthen and comfort those who desire your mercy and our intercession.

Be gracious and merciful to them. Pardon and forgive them for all the sins they have committed against you, whether this happened with or [29] without their awareness. Give them good intentions and thoughts, and make them well in body and soul. As far as this petition is not against your divine will, share your grace and mercy with the whole human race, and come to their help in all their needs.

O almighty Father in your eternal kingdom! we praise and thank you for your unspeakably wonderful grace and mercy; and for eternal salvation through your dearly beloved Son, our dear Lord and Savior Jesus Christ. We thank you, O Lord! for your bitter suffering and death, and the shedding of your innocent blood, which you have suffered and endured for us, so you might redeem and save us from eternal disgrace and torment. For this, O holy Father, and eternal Son of God, along with your Holy and good Spirit, we praise, honor, and glorify you most highly, above everything else, from now unto eternity! Amen. Amen.

✠ Yet Another Fine Prayer

O Lord, almighty God and heavenly Father! you who know and discern every human heart and flaw, I ask you, O holy Father in heaven! come to me with help and [30] comfort in my time of great distress. Forgive me my sins and misdeeds committed against you, whether in word or deed, in doing or leaving undone, with or without our awareness.

O Lord, my God! grant that I may know your holy Word, forgive me my grievous sins and transgressions, and do not charge me for my sins. This I pray from the bottom of my heart. O holy Father in heaven! do not bring your servant into judgment, but show me mercy. As a compassionate father shows mercy to his children, may you also be pleased to show mercy to me, a poor sinner.

O almighty God and heavenly Father! I pray from my heart, give me true faith, hope, and love, in which I can find salvation and redemption. Make me strong in my weakness, and vigorous in my illness, both in soul and body. So clothe me, O holy Father! with the armor of your divine strength, that I may endure against the deceitful onslaughts of the evil enemy, who fights against your truth. Give me also the shield of true, genuine faith, to maintain victory [31] over everything that might hinder me from living out your love and righteousness.

O holy Father in heaven! you heard the prayer of Elijah and of Paul. I plead that you will also hear my prayer and save me from everything wicked and evil. You enclosed Noah in the ark; enclose me also in the ark of the New Testament so my name may be found in the book of eternal life. This I pray, O merciful Father!

O holy Father in heaven! feed me with the living heavenly bread of your holy Word. Give me to drink the living water of your Holy Spirit. Look upon me always with your holy eyes, that I may turn away from evil. Protect me also from warfare and bloodshed, from the terrible war in the land, and from every form of confusion, which might deceive me and separate me from your love and righteousness.

O holy Father in heaven! do not let the petitions of your dear Child, Jesus Christ, be lost, nor the prayers of all believers made on my behalf.

O holy Father in heaven! I pray that you would also graciously protect me from acts of [32] terrible wickedness which cut a person off from the kingdom of heaven, such as adultery, fornication, impurity, lewdness, idolatry, sorcery, enmity, disputing, passion, anger, quarreling, division, schism, hate, murder, drunkenness, gluttony, and the like.[23]

O holy Father in heaven! protect me from these transgressions in a fatherly and gracious way, that I may be released and freed from them all. Purify and wash me with the living water, so that now and forevermore, I may truly pray, Our Father . . . [the Lord's Prayer].

☩

Yet Other Fine Prayers

The First Prayer
[For Grace Truly to Pray]

ᔕ Lord, almighty, eternal, benevolent, and gracious God, heavenly Father, who is merciful in Christ Jesus, our Lord! you are the one who best discerns and knows our every flaw and futility, that we are nothing and have nothing. Indeed, without your holy blessing, support, help, and grace, we could achieve nothing by ourselves except evil: every type of sin, iniquity, disgrace and transgression, vice, idleness and vanity, and every kind of evil deed of unholiness. For we certainly are nothing but [33] poor, miserable, sinful people by inclination, and poor, weak, unworthy, little earthworms,[24] on account of our sins.

Yet we ask you in complete humility and from the heart, O holy, dear Father in heaven, grant us grace that together we may truly call to you in prayer. Help us at all times, and give us your holy blessing, full of mercy, that we may be able to pray reverently, in spirit and in truth. May you hear and accept our prayer for your own sake, that it may serve for your credit and your high honor, praise, and glory. Let this be helpful to all of us gathered here, leading to our comfort, salvation, and eternal life.

And help us also, O holy Father of all grace, rich in love! that with genuine faith and honest hearts, we may utter the prayer which you yourself have taught us, O Lord Jesus Christ, rich in love, and have commanded us thus to pray: Our Father . . . [the Lord's Prayer].

✠

The Second Prayer
For Christian Virtues

O holy triune God in heaven, rich in love! We also pray from our whole heart, first and foremost, Build [34] us up, and plant us according to your holy will. Convert us and draw us graciously to you. Help us to obey you gladly and willingly, to serve you and follow in the ways of your commandments.

Oh! graciously equip us with true faith, with good hope and genuine Christian love, with honest faithfulness and truth. Graciously fill us as well with true, Spirit-filled knowledge of Jesus Christ and your holy Word and will. Grant us a genuine passion and love for everything good, through your holy and good Spirit. And on the other hand, grant us also a proper holy hate, ill-will, and abhorrence for everything evil, that we may hate what you hate and gladly love what you love.

Oh! graciously be our path and way, and at all times be our peace and guide, our refuge and haven. Set our hearts and minds constantly onto the path of your holy divine peace, that we may hold to you and serve you willingly as your dear children and servants, and do this forever, till the end of our poor and fleeting lives.

Give to us all, your own people, good intentions and thoughts, good understanding and holy knowledge, and good, holy desires. Indeed, also give us [35] forever a holy purpose, a holy will, a holy Christian zeal, and earnestness in everything good and holy, in whatever is pleasing and delightful to you.

Yes, give us holy health in soul and body, and also a holy desire and resolve according to the measure of your grace, as is pleasing to your divine wisdom. Indeed, if it is not against your holy and divine will for us so to pray, graciously distribute your rich and merciful goodness even to the whole human race, in accord with the pleasure of your holy will.

Come to us all, helping and comforting us in all our concerns and needs, both in soul and body. This we ask, O holy Father! for the sake of Jesus Christ. Amen.

✠

The Third Prayer
For the Forgiveness of Sins

We ask you, O holy Father of all mercies! graciously show us your mercy throughout the whole of our lives, and especially also right now, in these last and dangerous times. Forgive us all our sins and transgressions, both hidden and public, committed knowingly and unknowingly. [36]

Oh, pardon and forgive us for everything we have done against you, however we have sinned, whether it happened with or without our awareness, with words or with actions, secretly or openly, against our better judgment and conscience, against your law, and against your holy gospel. So we ask quite humbly and from our hearts, oh! be gracious and merciful to us, O holy Father! for the sake of Jesus Christ. Amen.

☩

The Fourth Prayer
Petition for All Kinds of Experiences of the Faithful Throughout the Whole of Christendom

We pray for all our fellow members, beloved brothers and sisters, wherever they may be, in all the corners and places of the whole world; whether they are gathered or scattered, suffering cross and distress, fettered and in prisons for your holy name's sake, or otherwise undergoing severe tribulation and affliction or life-threatening illness.

O! strengthen and console them everywhere, mercifully, with your wonderful holy grace. Graciously sustain them as well, through your holy and good Spirit, and your holy Word and [37] gospel. Do not let them depart from your truth, love, and righteousness, either to the right or to the left, until we have reached the end of our woeful life.

Oh! give this grace of yours to all who belong to you, that we will not be tempted by anything beyond our endurance. Instead, provide for us forever joyous paths that bypass all our troubles and times of persecution, according to your holy will.[25] And help us through your mercy, so that whatever you send our way, we may suffer and bear it all with true patience. [Amen.]

⳥

The Fifth Prayer
For Various People Suffering Afflictions

We pray, O compassionate Father! for all the sick, weak, and troubled souls, for all people in need, who suffer physical, mental, and spiritual afflictions. We pray for all devout widows and orphans, for all the evil-minded, the old, the infirm, and those becoming senile. Also help all the devout, those who are despairing, those met with ill will, those thrown into wretched prisons. In short, help all the distressed, afflicted, and anxious [38] who belong to your church throughout the whole wide world, in whatever circumstance or condition they may be found.

We also pray from our hearts for all people who belong to you, for all the concerns of your people for which we can still pray, and for those who heartily desire your grace and our petition. Give all of us your merciful, ever-helping hand, grace, comfort, hope, faith, and love. Strengthen all of us together in the genuine, true faith, in hope and patience, in true Christian love, faithfulness, and unity. Graciously unite us together in your noble, dear peace, O Father in heaven, rich in love, for the sake of Jesus Christ!

Receive and accept us mercifully into your holy covenant, and create in us your living and mighty holy Word, alive and active, which we daily hear, read, and contemplate. We also pray, oh! grant us grace that your Word might grow and increase in us daily, so you may find that it has grown and borne much fruit among us.

Help us to love you from our hearts, hanging onto you above all else. May we with true longing and desire serve you faithfully, as your dear children and servants, [39] until the end of our poor and fleeting life. [Amen.]

⚜

The Sixth Prayer
For All of Us Together

We pray, O holy, dear Father! graciously show us your mercy, as a father, full of love, shows mercy to his children. And keep sending down to us your holy angels, as loyal guides, that they may go before us, leading us and ever contending for us against all evil enticements. May your angels fight against all our enemies and opponents, saving us as well from the hands of every sort of ungodly enemy, those who envy, hate, and persecute us without cause.

From such enemies, mercifully protect us at all times, according to your holy will, until you have made us virtuous and able to overcome everything with patience, able to suffer and endure whatever you may have set before us.

Help us also that we do not depart from your holy Word, either to the right or to the left. Continue to prepare for us a path and way, a place and a home, peace [40] and a guide, that in all our dealings we may dwell safely among all our enemies. Look mercifully upon our many weaknesses, and lead us together in your name forever, to hear your holy Word in a useful and fruitful way. Continually draw us together in your mercy, under your powerful hand of grace, and under your fatherly care and protection. Take us under your divine grace and power, which cannot be overcome.

O holy, dear Lord God! concern yourself always for us, watch over and protect us. Do battle constantly for us, and fight mercifully for us all together, as long as we live. Give us obedient hearts, too, a craving and desire to act in accord with your holy will.

We also pray, O holy, dear Father! oh! be gracious and merciful to all of us, especially to us whom you have chosen through grace in Christ Jesus. Help us to long for you in all earnestness. Oh! with mercy forgive us also all our grievous vices, imperfections, and failings, according to your great goodness, rich in love.

Help us also, dear Lord God! that we may yet become worthy through your grace and Holy Spirit to flee all the misery that shall come upon all vain, [41] earthly worldlings, those who will be lost, and for whom you yourself do not wish [for us] to pray.

Protect us from such an outcome with your grace, O holy Father! Help us, instead, that we may truly belong in your church, that together we may rejoice in your kingdom, praising and lauding you into all eternity.

We ask you thus, O holy Father, oh! sanctify all our prayers, sighs, and utterances, through your holy and good Spirit, out of pure grace, for the sake of Jesus Christ. Amen.

⛪

The Seventh Prayer
Petition Against Schism

We ask you, holy Father! to show your grace and mercy to us all, throughout the whole wide world. Graciously draw us together with your blessing, care, and protection. Do not let division and disunity come among us.

Oh! may the false mob spirit which tears a group apart not be found among any of us, if this is not praying against your holy will. Instead, kindly safeguard us, O holy, dear Father! from every type of false doctrine and false living, from [42] every kind of mistrust and guile, from false faith and every sort of unkindness, and from every false idea and evil opinion. Indeed, safeguard us graciously from all that might damage or hinder our salvation and joy, that might divide us, or lead us away from your love and righteousness, or bring us to neglect your holy Word. [Amen.]

✠

The Eighth Prayer
For Those Fallen from Fellowship

Show mercy upon all those, O dear Lord, who have fallen away, who are frustrated and troubled, who have strayed from your love and righteousness and departed from your truth. Show compassion to those who have stumbled and committed major sins, or who otherwise through cross and affliction, anxiety and distress, have backslidden and fallen, and who still might again desire your grace and our prayers.

Oh! once more give them true understanding and knowledge, remorse and sorrow concerning their fall. Accept them [43] again graciously as your children and servants. Indeed, help them henceforth to love, fear, and honor you, and live in your presence. Grant them also the correct and true faith, through Jesus our Lord! [Amen.]

☩

The Ninth Prayer

For Faithful Shepherds, Teachers, and Preachers

We ask you, O Lord of the harvest, rich in love! oh! consider how the harvest is so very great, and the faithful workers are so few. O dear Lord! constantly raise up among us faithful teachers, good workers, and useful planters, in all places throughout the whole wide world.

In every corner and place, and in every age, give us such servants[26] in accord with your heart's desire. Call those who find grace before your eyes and are truly able to work, to proclaim and preach your holy Word and righteousness, without pride or deceit, without hypocrisy or false ambition. [44]

Through the thanksgiving of many devout people, may your holy name be honored and glorified. O Lord, rich in love! true God in heaven! create forever a sure path and entrance for your holy Word. Let it grow and multiply, and may it also be planted elsewhere as far as this is possible, that we all may be taught and instructed correctly. Feed and give drink to all who hunger and thirst after your kingdom and after your love and righteousness, according to your holy Word and gospel.

We also pray, O holy Father! for all faithful messengers, servants, and ministers whom you have sent out to proclaim and preach your holy Word and righteousness. Give each of them a holy mouth,[27] a holy wisdom, and a holy understanding, and may they be of good report, laying holy hands on others through your good Spirit. Let them declare your holy Word and righteousness, according to your holy will and pleasure.

We ask all this despite our great defects and pressing needs, so that all these things may also truly serve to the honor of your holy name and unto our eternal and temporal well-being, in body and soul. [Amen.] [45]

✠

The Tenth Prayer
For Political Authorities

We pray, O holy Father! for all types of people throughout the whole wide world, for whom it is still possible to pray. Protect especially all devout authorities throughout the whole wide earth. In particular, be merciful to all those under whom you have [put] your people.

Let not the hands of officials cause innocent blood to flow. Instead, give them grace to rule according to your holy will, for the purpose for which you have appointed them. May they plant and protect the good, and suppress and punish the evil. Thus may we and all those who fear your holy name lead a quiet and peaceful life here on earth. [Amen.]

✠

The Eleventh Prayer
For Our Enemies

Forgive all our enemies, those who can still be helped, as well as all the insulting and evil antagonists who do not know what they are doing, who are still hating us so much and [46] wishing evil upon us. They are continually mocking, oppressing, and persecuting us; lying and deceiving, and also mistakenly judging and damning us.

We pray for all of these whom you still want to convert and bring to grace. Forgive them all their sins and misdeeds, since they do not yet know what they are doing, nor are they aware of the shameful things they have done to us or might still do, before their conversion.

We ask this for the sake of your holy name. Do not hold this against them for our sakes, but convert them and us together, according to your holy will, as soon as it may please you. [Amen.]

✠

The Twelfth Prayer
Against the Ungodly Archenemies

We pray concerning all the ungodly archenemies whom you, O God! according to your eternal decree, perhaps are not willing to convert, and whom you have cast down into eternal damnation. Most graciously protect us from such people. Impede and restrain, shatter and destroy all their evil intentions. Make a shambles out of all their evil counsels and harsh attacks which they devise against you and your Word, as they rant and rave against your dear church and community.[28]

If this request is not [47] against your holy will, save us graciously from all godless, depraved persons! that they may not harm us, whether in body or in spirit. If this petition is not against your holy will, keep us from being corrupted by them. Instead, call us to true repentance, and save all whom you desire to bless. Convert all those whom you choose to convert. Assist all of us who are willing to be helped, that we before our departure will be able truly to repent of all our sins and transgressions. [Amen.]

✠
The Thirteenth Prayer
For the Loyal, Honest, and Good-hearted People

Be merciful, O dear Father! to all good and devout souls, to all the good, faithful, honest, good-hearted people who have shown genuine compassion to us through your grace. They have constantly come to us with caring help and protection, doing all this for the sake of your holy name.

O Lord, reward them abundantly with good blessings. Also give them everywhere what they lack and would like to have, from every holy and [48] good thing, whatever may promote your holy honor.

Forgive them all their sins and transgressions, and give them everything that is useful and needed, for soul and body. Just as you have been so gracious to us till now, we pray that you will not forsake us. Continue to protect and preserve us for the rest of our lives, graciously nourishing and keeping us, in body and soul.

Oh! give us as well a true, steadfast, and living faith, a genuine Christian love and uprightness, a good and blessed hope in you, O Lord! and also a steadfast trust in your goodness and great mercy. Also help us that from our whole heart and soul, we may keep this trust with you and with your holy Word. May we indeed love you from our hearts with all our strength, holding to you, and serving you truly until our final end, both in living and in dying.

Oh, protect us through your help and grace, that we do not separate ourselves from you so woefully, as do many poor, lost persons in the world who ask neither for you nor for your holy Word. Help us, instead, that we may be able to serve you truly, and have a heartfelt desire to hold to your commandments as long as we live, as much as is possible through your grace. [Amen.] [49]

✠

The Fourteenth Prayer
A Fine Prayer of Thanksgiving

We thank you humbly and from our hearts, and declare to you our deep praise, honor, and glory, and our highest thanksgiving, O Lord God, rich in love! We thank you for all your great deeds of kindness and fatherly faithfulness, and for your great gifts and acts of mercy which you have always shown to us and done for us, and especially now in these last, dark times.

We further extend our deep thanksgiving to you, O holy Father of all mercies! who has created everything, heaven and earth, the sea and everything therein! You keep faith forever[29] and create justice for those who often need to suffer much injustice. But you have also redeemed all those who have held to you throughout all time, who have believed, trusted, and served you truly, and have feared you constantly. [Amen.]

✠
The Fifteenth Prayer
[Thanksgiving for the Savior's Suffering]

🕭 highly praised Son of God! O faithful Savior of all those chosen throughout the world! O Lord, rich in love! we thank you with deep [50] humility. From our hearts we thank you for all your suffering and death, your merit and atonement, for all your unspeakable agony and torment, sufferings and the shedding of your innocent blood, even unto death.

You have borne all this and suffered death for us willingly and with great patience, through which you intend to redeem and save us from eternal disgrace and torment. For this, may you be highly praised into all eternity, O patient slaughtered Lamb![30] Amen.

✠
The Sixteenth Prayer
[Thanksgiving for God's Wonderful Grace]

🕭 holy, dear Father, reigning in your kingdom! we thank you once more and indeed offer you what you deserve, our greatest praise, honor, and glory. We declare our manifold and deepest thanks for all your unspeakably glorious goodness and acts of mercy, for all your blessings, spiritual and temporal gifts of grace, and deeds of kindness which cannot be counted.

From our hearts and in true humility, we also thank you for your holy, wonderful grace and loving mercy. And we especially thank you for your eternal salvation, which you have presented to us in Christ Jesus our Lord.

We also thank you from our hearts for all the times and opportunities [51] in which we can serve you and call on you and pray to you. Oh! holy God and Father! help us and make us able to conduct ourselves daily in your fear and to your holy honor. To this end, O holy triune Lord God, full of love, Father, Son, and Holy Spirit! may you be praised, honored, and glorified to the highest, in countless times of rich thanksgiving, from now into eternity. Amen. Our Father . . . [the Lord's Prayer].

✠

Prayer for Purity of the Heart

Oh! noble, holy, pure, unblemished Lord Jesus Christ! you Lover of purity, you are the crown of all honor and virtue! I lament and confess to you my heart's deep impurity. I have often defiled my body and soul through impure thoughts, words, and deeds.

Oh! you with a pure, gentle, and good heart, forgive me for these great sins of mine. Ward off from me the heavy punishment which you threaten upon those who are impure.

For blessed are the pure in heart; they shall see God. Thus without doubt the impure in heart will remain unblessed; they shall not see God. Therefore create in me, O God, a pure heart, and do not cast me away [52] from your holy face because of my impurity.[31]

I know that I cannot live a disciplined life, unless you give me such strength. That knowledge in itself is a deep grace. Hence, I humbly pray, sanctify and purify my heart through faith, through the Holy Spirit, repentance, and the new birth.[32] Strengthen me, that I may not allow the impure spirit to rule within me or to take over and own me, like an impure house. Let impurity not defile my soul, poison my thoughts, or pollute my body.

Extinguish in me the flames of lust, and gird up my loins and inner being with the girdle of purity. You, the Disciplinarian and noble Bridegroom of my soul, embrace my heart with your pure love; unite and marry my soul with your chaste heart. Fill my heart with holy and pure thoughts that through your love I may be a pure and unblemished member and remain thus forever.

So fill me that I will not become an impure vessel and member of Satan and a vessel of dishonor, but rather a vessel of grace and honor. May I not bury or lose my gifts, which you have lodged with me, as a vessel of mercy.

Through discipline and purification, may I separate myself from the unclean spirits, the [53] devil, and from all impure heathen. May I thus not be expelled from the new heavenly Jerusalem, but instead remain unified with you, being of one spirit, one heart, and one body with you. In holy baptism you have washed and dedicated me, anointed and healed me with the Holy Spirit, and sanctified me as your holy temple and dwelling place.[33]

Oh! teach me to bear in mind that my body is a temple and dwelling of your Holy Spirit, so that I do not destroy God's temple, and you in turn destroy me. Show me that I am a member of Christ and dare not turn myself into a dishonorable member, sinning against my own body.

O noble, chaste, disciplined heavenly Bridegroom,

who feasts under the roses of purity, feed my soul with your knowledge and pure love. Drive out of me every evil thought, so you with your Holy Spirit may dwell in me and the holy angels may remain with me forever. Amen.

✠

Another Prayer

O almighty God and heavenly Father! you know and are aware of all human hearts and needs. We pray, O holy Father [54] in heaven! give us your grace that we together may call upon you and pray in the name of your dear Child, Jesus our Savior, so that we may truly say, Our Father . . . [the Lord's Prayer].

O almighty God and heavenly Father! we pray, have mercy upon us and come to us with help and comfort in these dangerous last times. O Father! we ask you, allow our prayers to come before you, and hear our call.

So we pray, O Father! in the name of Jesus Christ our Savior, pardon and forgive us all our sins and transgressions, however we have acted against your will, whether this happened in word or deed, by what was done or left undone.

Thus we ask you, now show us mercy as a compassionate father over his children. Do not punish us in accord with what we deserve, but alongside temptation provide a merciful escape, so we may be able to emerge victorious. Where you have given us much to suffer, give us patience in equal measure.[34]

So we ask now, O Father! clothe us with the genuine, true faith, with your true love, faithfulness, and truth, and with the power of your Holy Spirit. Above all things may we honor, fear, and love you, O Father! with our whole heart, with the desire of our souls, with [55] willing hearts and minds, and keep your commandments until the end of our lives. This we ask in the name of our Lord Jesus Christ.

We also pray, O holy Father! that you might show us the petition of your dear Child, Jesus Christ, protecting us from all evil, and keeping us in your truth and in your holy name. Thus may we all be one, O Father! we in you and you in us, so that your holy Word may remain in us, keeping the unity of your Holy Spirit through the bond of your peace.[35] This we pray in the name of your dear Son, Jesus Christ.

And so we pray, O heavenly Father! create for your holy Word a path and a way alongside all tribulation. Lead us together in your holy name, and do not permit us to become scattered and forsaken like sheep who have no shepherd. Instead, may you consider how great is the harvest, but how few are the workers. Thus we pray, O Lord of the harvest, raise up workers for your harvest, faithful shepherds and teachers, servants[36] after your holy heart.

Call those who have found grace in your holy eyes, who will proclaim your holy Word without a trace of [56] pride but through the grace and power of your Holy Spirit. May that preaching serve to the praise and honor of your holy name, and for the benefit and salvation of your church.

So we pray, O heavenly Father! for our dear brothers and sisters who stand within your truth, whom you know, for you know your own, O Lord. Wherever they may be, may you gather them at the given time from the four winds, from one end of heaven to the other. So we pray, O Father! for every person who is sick, imprisoned, or old, for everyone with a troubled and distressed heart, and for widows and orphans. Grant them grace and patience equal to their need and burden, to trust confidently in your grace and mercy until they reach a blessed end.

We also pray, holy, righteous Father! for all good-hearted people who show us compassion with food and drink, with home and refuge. O Lord! may you be highly praised that you prepared them for such acts of kindness. May you, O Lord! reward them here in this life, and there in eternal life.

We also pray for all people who call upon your holy name with a repentant heart, who in their hearts acknowledge and confess their failings and weaknesses, who from their hearts desire your grace and the petitions of the faithful. [57]

May you, Lord in heaven! be gracious to us and help all people to do justice, since you know the hearts of all people. For you alone know the hearts of all people, their minds and thoughts, their intentions. Indeed, all mysteries are revealed in the light of your countenance.

So grant us wisdom from above, O Lord! that from our hearts we can fear you in all things.

We pray, O Lord of all lords and King of all kings! for the kings and all authorities. Let them fear you in their hearts, so they do not misuse the power which you have given them. Instead, may they use it to protect and care for the devout, and to frighten and punish the evildoers and the unjust. Thus may all those who fear you from their hearts lead a peaceful and quiet life, in pleasant peace and unity.

We also pray, O Lord, for the human race throughout the whole world, for all people, if this petition is not against your divine will. We also pray for our enemies who hate us and do not know what they are doing. If it is not against your will, grant them strength to acknowledge their sins, that they will be able to repent.

So we pray, O heavenly Father, for all of us who stand in your truth. Bind us together in the bond of your love, [37] for your love [58] is the true bond by which you call together your chosen ones under your care and protection and divine grace and power, which cannot be overcome.

Hence we pray, O Father! guide our feet, heart, mind, and being onto the path of your divine peace, for you are a God of love, unity, and peace, and not of division.

So we pray, O holy Father! in the name of your dear Child, Jesus Christ, send into our hearts your Holy Spirit as Comforter, as a pledge and seal of the correct, true faith and your divine love.

May this Spirit comfort us in all our troubles and lead us, O Father! in your truth, so we do not go astray, either to the left or to the right. Instead, make your holy Word, which you have given us to know, fruitful in our hearts. At our time of reckoning, may you find your Word multiplied among us. This we pray, O Father! in the name of Jesus Christ, our Lord and Savior.

O heavenly Father! we praise and thank you for your great gifts and deeds of mercy, for food and drink, for house and shelter, and for all that is good. Indeed, all good gifts come from you alone. So we pray, O [59] Lord!

almighty God! remove from us everything which oppresses us, those sins which cling to us, such as anger, stub-
bornness, envy, hate, immorality, pride, and greed, the
root of all evil.[38]

Take from us hearts inclined toward evil, and all forms
of injustice. Create in us pure hearts, and renew in us an
honest and willing spirit. Teach us your paths, and give us
grace, O Lord! that we may walk in them.

This we pray, O Lord! to you who have created everything, heaven and earth, the sea and everything in it and
on it. You keep faith forever[39] and create justice for all
people who suffer injustice. You have saved all who from
their hearts have placed their faith and trust in you. Since
you will continue to save such people, give us grace that
we also may be able to place our faith and trust in you.

O Father, grant us the love which flows from a pure
heart, a good conscience anchored in your Holy Spirit,
and a sincere faith. We ask you, O Father! to strengthen
us now in our fight and sustain us in our sickness, whether
in soul or body.

Clothe us now, O Father! with the armor of your
divine strength, so we may withstand the deceitful ad-
vances of the evil [60] enemy, who fights against truth.
Give us also the shield of true faith, to maintain victory
over all that may hinder us from experiencing your righteousness. Place on our heads the helmet of your salvation, that we need not fear any human being, who with-
ers like the grass. Instead, may we fear you, O Lord, since
you search out human hearts and test our inner being.[40]

So now place into our hearts the sword of your Holy
Spirit, which is your holy Word and Spirit. Thus may we

stand firmly for your holy name and fight for the truth up to the time of our blessed end. Let us then be found as true witnesses of your holy Word, so our names will be found in your book of eternal life. May we be worthy through your wonderful grace to flee the coming evil and your bitter wrath, and to appear joyfully before your holy face.

Indeed, O Lord Jesus Christ! may you be a gracious judge for us, so that with your chosen children we may rejoice in your eternal kingdom, praising your holy name forever and ever. This we pray, O Father! in the name of your dear Son, our Lord Jesus Christ. Amen. [61]

O heavenly Father! we declare our praise and thanksgiving to you for your unspeakably wonderful grace, and for your immeasurably great love which you have shown us through Jesus Christ, our Lord and Savior. You, O Lord Jesus Christ! have purchased and redeemed us with your holy and precious merit on the cross, on which you allowed your holy body to be broken and your holy blood to be shed. For us sinners, you thereby became a pure sacrifice, holy and perfect. We could have been redeemed through no other sacrifice than through your bitter suffering and death. In your great love, you so willingly have suffered for us, in hope and faith.

May you on the day of the last judgment again awaken us through the pure grace of your great mercy. Be an advocate for your children, and bring us with you into your eternal kingdom, O holy Father! along with your dear Child, Jesus Christ and your saints! One Lord! almighty God! may your holy, lofty, and all-powerful name be highly praised, honored, glorified, and blessed, from now through all eternity. Amen. [62]

⊹

A Fine Prayer

O Lord! almighty, good, merciful, and heavenly God and Father and Lord of heaven and earth! we come again to you as your children. We pray, O holy Father! give us your grace from above, that we may be able to call to you and worship you in spirit and in truth, in faith and with the pure and true love of God, in wisdom and in the fear of God, in humility and submission.

We faithfully pray, O holy Father! forgive us for all the sins we have committed against you, whether they happened in our minds or thoughts, with words or deeds. Eternal God and Father! you certainly recognize and know all this already. We are sorry for them from our hearts, and we confess before you that we are poor, sinful human beings. Indeed, we are not worthy to be called your children. Without your help and grace, we do not possess the strength even to think good thoughts, much less to act aright.

So we faithfully pray, O holy Father! through your grace forgive us all the sins we have committed, for the sake of your wonderful grace and mercy.

We faithfully pray, O holy Father! protect us also from all future sins. [63] Give us grace that henceforth we may no longer sin, indeed, that we may do nothing against your holy and divine Word and will.

We faithfully pray, O holy Father! place in our hearts wisdom and reason from above, that we may properly acknowledge our sins and then avoid them. May we thus mend our ways and repent.

We pray, O holy Father! strengthen our faith, increase

our love, and align our hearts with the true and pure love
of God and the patience of Jesus Christ. May we live and
walk at all times in the path of peace and your divine
love. May we not desire anything more than you, O Lord!
and your holy and divine Word, your law, and your righteousness.

We pray, O holy Father! give us grace that we may
love you above all things, from our whole heart and from
our soul's desire, and with all our strength and might.

We faithfully pray, O holy Father! give us grace that
we also may love our neighbor as ourself. May we choose
to treat others as we would like them to treat us. And
whatever we do not want others [64] to do to us, may we
also refrain from doing the same to them.[41]

We faithfully pray, O holy Father! grant us grace that
we may guard ourselves against every injustice, against all
conceit and pride, greed and selfishness, bickering and
crusading, animosity and dissension.

Protect us from all discord, and pour into our hearts the
perfect divine love. Grant us grace that we, above everything else, may strive first of all for the kingdom of God
and for your divine righteousness.[42] So with patience in
good works, may we wholeheartedly strive for eternal life.

We pray, O holy Father! show us mercy, and through
grace come to us with help and comfort. Protect us also
from temporal and eternal torment and pain. Shield us
from every disgrace and shame. Destroy and shatter every
evil counsel and charge which has been or might be lev-
eled against your Word and will, and against your people.

We faithfully pray, O holy Father! bind us together
with a bond of peace and with your pure divine love, that

no one may tear us apart or destroy us. [65] Grant us your mercy, and do not judge us with your wrath, but be gracious to us, and merciful.

We faithfully pray, O holy Father! give us also a place in your kingdom, for it lies in your power to grant this. With you there is no lack, and all your storerooms are full. Heaven and earth must yield to your great almighty power. So through grace, take us to yourself, into your kingdom.

We faithfully pray, O holy Father! protect us also from every future sin. Give us grace that we may grow in goodness each day and hour, and also that we may be able to abide therein, even to the end of our life.

We faithfully pray, O holy Father! keep us from perishing along the way. Instead, give us your grace that we may enter life's battle with your holy Word and will. Thus may we fight a good fight and complete the course, maintaining the faith according to your holy and divine will and pleasure.[43] May we grow and increase in goodness each day and hour, and persevere in it until the end of our life. [66]

We faithfully pray, O holy Father! hear our prayer. Hear us just as you have heard all the devout who have passed away, indeed, just as you heard Susanna and Judith, and also the old Eliezar with his companions. Save us and redeem us, just as you saved Daniel in the lions' den, and Jonah in the belly of the whale.

We faithfully pray, O holy Father! keep us in your holy, divine care and protection, just as in the fiery furnace you kept the three companions Shadrach, Meshach, and Abednego fresh and healthy.[44] You are so rich that your streams overflow their banks with grace. Therefore, we faithfully ask you, give us grace that we may serve and hold to you firmly and unswervingly. May we never, never give in to injustice, and never forsake your holy commandments, so that we do not stray, either to the right or to the left.

We faithfully pray, O holy Father! do not permit us to give in to weakness or timidity. Take from us all timidity and weakness, of which sadly much can be found among us. May we not be tempted by our possessions. [67] Instead, always provide a gracious escape alongside temptation and distress.[45]

If it is your will that we suffer, then at the same time give us sufficient faith, patience, comfort, and love. Give us the grace so to live and walk that we may be found to be your constant servants who can wait for their Lord. Thus, O Lord! whenever you start the wedding banquet, may you find us equipped and prepared each day and hour.

We faithfully pray, O holy Father! do not take life from us until you are reconciled and satisfied with us. Allow us to die a death pleasing to you, and give us nothing but your grace, that we may awaken with the wise virgins.[46] May we with all our hearts meditate on things above, not on what is on the earth, so that all together we may truly be spiritually minded and of the same courage and mind. May we call to you with united voice from our whole heart, saying in spirit and in truth, Our Father . . . [the Lord's Prayer].

Since everything rests in your hand and power, O holy Father! we ask you to be our help and comfort, our refuge

[68] and protection, and our confidence in all things, our counsel and counselor, our path and guide.

Direct our hearts in the way of peace, so we may have peace with all people, as far as it is possible for us. May we love our enemies, bless those who curse us, and do good in return for the evil inflicted upon us. Also help us gladly to share our homes and lodging with others, feed the hungry, give drink to those who thirst, shelter guests, clothe the naked, and visit the sick and imprisoned, as much as you demand from us.[47]

We faithfully pray, O holy Father! also grant us grace that we always may strive for peace, for salvation and love, without which no one shall see the Lord.

We also pray, O holy Father! give us grace always to live and walk inoffensively among Jews and Gentiles, and among God's gathered people, indeed, also among all people in the whole wide world.

We faithfully pray, O holy Father! for this small congregation, and also for everyone within your whole church, wherever they may be found. We especially pray for the aged, the sick, and those imprisoned; for all sorrowing and oppressed hearts and souls; [69] indeed, for all people who have lost their understanding, who are heavy of mind, anxious, depressed, timid, and filled with worry. We pray for all who are burdened and laden for the sake of your holy and divine Word and name. Give them and all of us together a good outcome and a blessed end.

We pray, O holy Father! for all who have departed from your Word and will, and from the truth. Give them grace that they again may return and repent. If it is not against your holy and divine will for us so to pray, then through your goodness and graciousness, raise them up and accept them once again into the service of your divine righteousness, indeed, into the knowledge of your eternal truth.

Oh! make it possible for all people to repent, those who from the heart desire to mend their ways, so that none might miss out on your grace.

We pray, O Lord! for all truehearted people who recognize your Word and will. May they respond also with correct understanding to your holy Word and will. Grant them the true new birth from above in their hearts.

We ask, O holy Father! that you note the misery within this world, and how great the harvest [70] is, yet how few are the faithful workers. Prepare us all as faithful workers, and also send us leaders[48] for your harvest, shepherds and teachers, servants and messengers. Call leaders[49] who have been taught and commissioned by you, whom you have also blessed and filled with your Holy Spirit.

Send those who are able and virtuous in proclaiming your holy and divine Word: pure, unadulterated, and genuine, without arrogance and pride, without haughtiness and selfishness. Through these leaders and through your grace, may people everywhere be built up and restored. May the souls of many people escape eternal anxiety through your grace. Let the number of holy, chosen children of God be built up and restored through your servants. Mold us into a holy people, into a people of character, that we may proclaim the power of your eternal truth.

We also faithfully pray, O heavenly Father! for our

children, indeed, for all children, all children for whom you desire our prayers. Give them wisdom and understanding in their hearts, and give them the ability to acknowledge your Word and will. May they learn to know and hold to your Word and will with their whole heart. Draw them with the tug of your [71] mercy unto the knowledge of your eternal truth. Otherwise, take them from this life in their childhood.[50]

We pray, O holy Father! that injustice not be multiplied through us or our children. Instead, give us grace to raise our children in true Christian virtues, disciplining them without any bitterness and without anger. Through their efforts and ours, may the number of your holy, chosen children of God be built up and strengthened.

We faithfully pray, O holy Father! grant us grace that we may raise our children in genuine Christian virtues. May we be good examples, showing them the way in word, life, and conduct. Through our life and conduct, may they also be built up and strengthened. May the number of your holy, chosen children of God also be multiplied and fulfilled through us and our children.

We faithfully pray, O holy Father! for our fathers and mothers, brothers and sisters, indeed for all friends and relatives, also for all those we know, and for those we do not know. Through grace, come to them with help for what they most need and most urgently lack. [72]

We pray, O holy Father! for all our enemies, who hate, insult, and persecute us. Do not hold this against them as evil for our sakes. If it is not praying against your holy will, let them experience repentance and a time of grace. Grant all people repentance, those who from the heart desire to repent and mend their ways.

We pray, O holy Father! for all truehearted people who speak well of us and assist us with food, drink, and housing. O Lord, we pray, reward them with goodness now, and even much more in life eternal.

We also pray for the whole human race, for kings and all authorities, and especially for those under whom your people are dwelling. Give them wisdom and understanding, that they may rule with peace, guard and protect the faithful, and also judge and prevent evil. Thus may they perform their office and service as you have determined and ordained.

We pray, O holy Father! also grant us grace that we may continue to dwell under human authorities and be permitted to live out a devout, God-fearing life and [73] existence on the path of righteousness and truth. Indeed, grant that others may come to know that our friendliness goes out to all people, and that we dwell among them peacefully and with upright character.

May we radiate and shine as a light in the world. When others see our pure walk in Christ, may they also be won over, encouraged, and strengthened—through the example of our life and walk, even without verbal witness. May this all serve your holy, divine name in praise and glory, and allow us as well to experience solace, salvation, and eternal life, through Jesus Christ our Lord. Amen.[51]

O Lord, almighty God and heavenly Father! we praise and thank you truly and most deeply for all your faithfulness and love, so great, which you continue to reveal and demonstrate each day and hour. O Lord! may you be praised now and from everlasting to everlasting.

We so deeply and truly declare to you our praise and thanksgiving, O holy Father! for all of your wonderful grace and mercy, for your beloved Son's bitter suffering and death, also that he shed his holy and innocent blood. We praise you for your fatherly mercy, indeed, for all your most worthy gifts and acts of grace which you have revealed and demonstrated to us. Therefore, may [74] your holy name be praised and glorified from everlasting to everlasting.

We faithfully pray, O holy Father! grant us also growth and maturity, and make your Word living and strong in our hearts. Thus may your holy Word also bear fruit in our hearts, unto the praise and glory of your most holy name, as well as for the needs and consolation of our poor souls.

O holy Father! we also utter truly our highest praise and thanksgiving to you for good health, which you have provided and given us, and also for our good place in this land, for house and shelter. We thank you for all your holy and worthy gifts and acts of grace which you have shown and provided for us each day and hour. May you be praised now and from everlasting to everlasting.

We faithfully pray, O holy Father! watch over everything we possess, over everything useful and good for us, for both soul and body.

We faithfully pray, O holy Father! bless us in our going out and coming in. Keep our mouths and tongues, our hearts and beings, and set our hearts upon the path of your holy and divine peace. [75]

We faithfully pray also, O holy Father! protect us from

flood, fire, and every major disaster, from times of evil, from false rumors, from all evil ties, from every worldly encumbrance and dishonor.[52] Protect us from everything which might harm or bring damage to soul and body.

We pray, O holy Father! bind us together with the bond of peace and with your pure, divine love. Thus may we be able to live and conduct ourselves with our whole heart, solely within your holy and divine Word and will, and do so from now on, even to the end of our lives.

This we pray, O holy Father! in the name of your beloved Son, Jesus Christ, our Lord. Amen, Amen.

☦

Prayer and Consolation
For Those Exiled and Persecuted
Because of Their Confession of the Truth

Oh, faithful God, sole refuge of the forsaken! listen to us in accord with your wonderful righteousness. God, our Salvation, you are the refuge for everyone upon the earth, as well as far away on the sea. You are our shelter forever and ever. Even before the [76] mountains existed, before the earth and the world were created, you are, O God, from everlasting to everlasting.[53]

Have mercy upon us in our distress. Behold, nowhere does the world want to tolerate us. We continue to be persecuted, and we have no fixed home. What was said by our Savior, Christ Jesus, is being fulfilled with us: Behold, I am sending you out like sheep into the midst of wolves. You must be hated by everyone for my name's sake. Whoever endures to the end will be saved.[54] Oh!

dear Father, may we in genuine patience and perseverance endure to the end.

Since it also is said of us, If they persecute you in one
town, flee to another,[55] we thus have this hope and comfort. With these words, you have appointed a home for us
and will be at our side in our flight, as you were with the
infant Jesus, and with the patriarch Jacob when God's
host [of angels] met him.[56]

Oh! Lord Jesus Christ! may your example comfort us,
where you say, If the world hates you, know that it earlier hated me. Disciples are not above their master. I have
chosen you from the world; therefore the world hates
you.[57]

So grant us patience, since the world cannot be otherwise, and since all who want to live a godly life in you, O
Christ! must suffer persecution.[58] Grant us grace that we
may [77] patiently take upon ourselves the cross, consid-
ering the example of the holy apostles, as Saint Paul re-
counts: I think that God considers us apostles as the very
least within the human race, having given us over to
death. For we have become a spectacle to the world, and
to angels, and to other people. To this very hour we suffer hunger and thirst, and are naked and beaten, having
no certain home. When we are reviled, we bless; when we
are persecuted, we endure it; when we are slandered, we
flee. We are always like a curse to the world, like refuse
swept out for all people to stomp on.[59]

O Lord Christ! let your Word be our consolation,
where you say, Blessed are those who are persecuted for
the sake of righteousness, for the kingdom of heaven is
theirs. Blessed are you when people revile and persecute

you for my sake and speak every sort of evil against you, thus spreading their lies. Be joyful and comforted; you will be well rewarded in heaven. For thus they persecuted the prophets who lived before your time.[60]

Oh! Lord God! let the word of the holy apostle Paul also be our comfort: We are persecuted, but we are not forsaken. And again: We must through much affliction enter the kingdom of God.[61]

Let us also reflect on the friendly words of St. Peter, where he says, [78] Rejoice that you are suffering with Christ, so that you also may have joy and bliss when his glory is revealed. Blessed are you when you are reviled on account of the name of Christ, for the Spirit of God's glory rests on you; among them, God is blasphemed, but among you, he is glorified.[62]

O God! how great a consolation it is for all your joyful witnesses, where you say, Whoever touches you, touches the apple of my eye. Therefore, we hope you will protect all your pilgrims, and those among us who are forced into affliction, like an apple of the eye. Shelter them under the shadow of your wings.[63] Be with us wherever we are, accompany us, and care for us. For the earth is the Lord's and the fullness thereof; the world, and all that dwells therein.[64]

Lord! your grace extends as far as the heavens and your truth as far as the clouds. Take note of our flight [from persecution]. Gather our tears into your pocket; without a doubt you are counting them. Blessed is the one whose help comes from the God of Jacob, whose hope rests in the Lord God, who created heaven, earth, the sea, and everything in it, who keeps faith forever, who metes out justice for those who suffer violence and injustice, who feeds the hungry.

The Lord redeems the imprisoned, the Lord opens the [79] eyes of the blind. The Lord raises up those who have been struck down. The Lord loves the righteous. The Lord protects the strangers and orphans, keeps the widows, and turns back the way of the ungodly. The Lord is king forever, your God, O Zion, for all generations. Hallelujah! Amen.[65]

⛫

Prayer About Christian Discipleship

Oh! most gracious and compassionate Lord Jesus Christ, rich in love! Most gentle, humble, patient Lord! What a beautiful example of a holy life, rich in virtue, you have provided for us. Now we are to follow in your footsteps.

You are an unspotted mirror of all virtue, a perfect example of salvation, a faultless standard of faithfulness, a sure plumb line of righteousness.[66] Oh, how absolutely my sinful life contrasts with your holy life!

Although I am to live in you as a new creature, I am living rather in the old creation, in Adam, instead of in you, my dear Lord Jesus Christ! I ought to live according to the Spirit, but sadly, I am living according to the flesh, and I know that Scripture says, If you live according to the flesh, you will die.[67]

Oh! you compassionate, patient, long-suffering Lord! forgive [80] me my sins, cover up my defects, overlook my misdeeds, and close your holy, tender eyes to my impurity. Cast me not away from your countenance. Do not expel me from your house as one who is impure and a leper. From my heart remove all pride, which is the devil's weed. Plant in me your humility as the root and foundation of virtue. Root out every bit of vengeance, and grant me your great gentleness. Oh! you highest jewel of all virtue, beautify my heart with pure faith, with fervent love, with living hope, with holy devotion, with childlike awe.

O my sole refuge! my love and my hope! my honor, my jewel! your life has been nothing but love, gentleness, and humility.

Therefore, allow your noble life to be in me, too. May your virtuous life also be my life. Let me be one spirit, one body, and one soul with you, that I may live in you and you in me. May you live in me, and not I in myself.[68] Grant that I might so acknowledge and love you, that I may walk just as you have walked.

If you are my light, then shine in me. If you are my life, then live in me. If you are my jewel, then adorn me with beauty. If you are my [81] joy, then rejoice in me. If I am your dwelling place, then take full possession of me. May I totally be your instrument, that my body, my soul, and my spirit may be holy.

You, Eternal Way, lead me! You, Eternal Truth, teach me! You, Eternal Life, revive me! Keep me from being the instrument of an evil spirit, that through me and in me, he does not exercise and carry out his evil, his lies, arrogance, greed, wrath, and filthiness. For such is the image of Satan, from which you want to save me, O beautiful, perfect Image of God.[69]

Instead, each day renew my body, spirit, and soul after

your image, until I am perfect. Let me die to the world, that I may live unto you. Let me rise with you, that I may ascend heavenward with you. Let me be crucified with you, that I may come to you and enter into your glory. Amen.[70]

✚

Prayer About the Kingdom of Christ

Lord Jesus Christ! King of honor, grace, and glory, I lament and confess to you with true regret and sorrow that I, alas, have been serving the prince of this world in Satan's kingdom, with the works of darkness. Indeed, the evil enemy has been reigning in me, [82] wickedly holding me prisoner through sin.

Oh, my Lord Jesus! how terrible it is that this strong one, armed to the hilt, thus maintains his palace within poor human beings. I thank you, however, from my heart, that you have made me able to share in the inheritance of the saints in the light, and have rescued me from the power of darkness, and transferred me into your kingdom, in which I have salvation through your blood, the forgiveness of sins.[71]

Through the blood of the covenant and eternal testament, you have led your prisoners from the pit in which there is no water, and you have made a new, eternal covenant with me.[72] Help me remain steadfast therein. Gather more and ever more people into your kingdom. Confirm your work, and give increase within your kingdom that many people may be transformed.

Enter us, as your citizens, into the book of your heavenly city—indeed, into your hands. Keep us, that we may remain eternally as partners in your kingdom. We have given you our names in baptism, we have passed over into your covenant, and we have granted you our allegiance.

Oh! King of grace, come into my heart. Come softly, and gently shield my heart from all unrest. You came to this world in poverty; come and make me humble and poor in spirit. Thus may I bear suffering for the sake of my sins [83], and hunger and thirst after your righteousness, that I may be eternally rich in you.

O Righteous One, come to me, a miserable sinner, and make me righteous. Clothe me with your righteousness, since God has made you my righteousness, sanctification, and redemption.[73]

Come, King of Peace! give me a peaceful, quiet conscience, and align me with your eternal peace and eternal calm. Make me gentle, merciful, and pure of heart.

Come, King of Mercies! fill me here in this life with your mercy, so that you may fill me there with your eternal glory. In this, your kingdom of grace, rule over me with your Holy Spirit. Indeed, establish your kingdom in me, which is righteousness, peace, and joy in the Holy Spirit.[74]

Illuminate my heart, purify my life, sanctify my thoughts, that they may be reverent and pleasing to you. Enfold me in your grace that I may never fall away.

Come to us, Holy Trinity! Renovate us as your dwelling and temple, and kindle in us the light of your knowledge, faith, love, hope, humility, patience, prayer, perseverance, and fear of God.

Grant that within our souls we may dwell constantly

in heaven [84] and yearn for your glory. And just as here in this world, you rule and love the kingdom of your divine power and omnipotence, so also be the mighty Lord-Protector of your spiritual kingdom and your church.

Remain with us, Lord Jesus Christ! according to your promise, every day until the end of the world. Do not forsake your children and your church as orphans; otherwise they have no father on earth.

Lord, our Ruler! spread your glorious name throughout the earth, so that there is thanksgiving to you in heaven. May you, in accord with the praise celebrated through the mouths of babes and infants, pass judgment, so that you may destroy the enemy and the avenger.[75]

You, O Lord Christ! are the fairest among those who inhabit the earth. Most gracious are your lips, for which God has blessed you eternally.

Gird your sword to your side, O Mighty One, and clothe yourself in majesty, for in your radiance you will conquer. Move the truth forward for the good, to obtain justice for those in misery. Thus will your right hand perform miracles. Your arrows are sharp, so even kings prostrate themselves before you, in the midst of the enemies of the King.

God! may your throne remain forever and ever. The scepter of your kingdom is an upright scepter. You love righteousness and hate ungodliness. Therefore your God has anointed you, O Lord Christ, with [85] the oil of joy beyond all your companions.

Each time you step out of your ivory palace in your beautiful splendor, you are clothed with pure myrrh, aloe, and cassia.[76] You are the King of Glory, strong and powerful. The Lord is powerful in battle. Make wide the gates, and raise high the doors in the world, that the King of Glory may enter.[77]

To you, God has said, Sit at my right side, until I make your enemies a footstool for your feet. The Lord will send the scepter of your kingdom from Zion. May you rule in the midst of your enemies! After your victory, your people in holy attire will be ready to bring sacrifices to you.

Your children will be born unto you as the dew rising in the dawn of morn. The Lord has sworn, and he will not regret his promise. You are a priest forever, after the order of Melchizedek.[78]

Praised be the one who comes in the name of the Lord, the Lord God, who enlightens us. O Lord, help! O Lord, grant us victory! You have removed sin, curse, and death, and have blessed us with an eternal blessing, with heavenly possessions. Give to your people strength, power, and victory against all spiritual and physical enemies.

And since you are also a King of Glory, make us citizens in your kingdom of glory. When you come in your [86] great power and glory, and all the holy angels with you, you will be sitting on the throne of your glory. Fill us then with those words of joy: Father, I desire that those also, whom you have given to me, may be with me where I am, so that they may see my glory. Come here, you who have been blessed by my Father, inherit the kingdom which has been prepared for you from the beginning! Amen.[79]

✠

Prayer for Comfort During Physical Poverty

Merciful, gracious God, dear Father! you have laid upon me the cross of physical poverty, no doubt for my own good. Grant me patience to carry this cross well and to submit myself obediently to your gracious will. For everything comes from you: happiness and unhappiness, poverty and wealth, life and death. You create poverty, and you create wealth. You bring low, and you lift up.[80]

Show me, however, faithful God! the honest means and ways to feed myself and my family. Bless my vocation and my work. You have indeed said that all poor people are to feed themselves with the labor of their own hands.[81]

May this blessing also come upon me. Grant that my family and I may eat from your kind fatherly hand, like the birds [87] of the sky, who neither sow nor reap. Yet you, heavenly Father, feed them. Each year you clothe the lilies and flowers of the field with new robes. Indeed, each year you grant every creature a new body after its kind. You also will certainly not forget me and my family, for you, heavenly Father! know what all we need.

Hence, teach me above everything else to seek your kingdom and your righteousness, so that in line with your promise, you will fulfill my temporal needs as well.[82] Here on earth I have no human consolation, for no one is a friend of the poor. Therefore, may you yourself be my consolation, you who are called the refuge and strength of the poor and lowly.

May my poverty not lead me to do evil or use forbidden means. Instead, may it lead to a stronger faith and trust in you, and to every Christian virtue of humility, gentleness, patience, prayer, hope, and perseverance.

Grant that in my poverty I will not be a burden to anyone. But prepare for me voluntary benefactors whom you love, and endow them with every grace. Oh, dear God! the one who is poor is like a stranger on earth, whom no one wants to acknowledge, in whom no one takes an interest.

This, however, is my consolation: you have said, You shall [88] befriend the orphans and widows and strangers, and give them food and clothing, and stand in fear of the Lord your God.[83] So this also is my comfort: it is written, The Lord raises the thirsty from the dust, and lifts high the poor from the filth, placing them among the princes, and letting them inherit the throne of honor.[84] You, dear Father! have thus ordained that the rich and the poor must dwell together. Yet you, Lord! have made them all.

Therefore, dear Father! accept me also, and allow no injustice or act of violence to fall on me, so that I will not be crushed. You yourself say, It is better to be poor and walk devoutly, than to be rich and walk in perverse ways.[85]

Help me to keep in mind what the aged Tobias said to his son: We are certainly poor, but we shall have great wealth if we fear God, avoid sins, and do good.[86] And David says, The little which a righteous person possesses is better than the great wealth of many an ungodly person. I was young, and have become old, and have yet to see a righteous person forsaken, or his offspring begging for bread.[87]

With this promise I am comforted and content. Thus it is better to have little and be [89] righteous, than to have a large income and live unjustly. For we have brought nothing into the world, and we shall take nothing with us out of the world.[88]

Therefore I pray to you for such a heart that concerns itself more with eternal wealth than with temporal goods. You will certainly grant me my modest portion. Let me follow the beautiful teaching of the most-wise house preacher, who says, Trust God, and remain in your vocation, for it is very easy for the Lord to make a poor person rich.[89]

Let me look upon the example of my Savior, Jesus Christ, who says, birds of the sky have their nests, and foxes have their holes, but the Son of Man does not even have a place to lay his head.[90]

You, Lord, are my wealth and my portion. You preserve my inheritance. You fill my heart with joy, even though others may have much wine and grain. I am poor and wretched. However, the Lord cares for me. I hope that I may also see the goodness of the Lord in the land of the living. Be comforted and courageous, you who wait confidently for the Lord.[91]

God, you have created me to praise you. Grant that I may love you worthily. You are the most majestic, the one most worthy of praise, the most holy, the most righteous, the most beautiful, the most gracious, the most friendly, indeed, you are the one most true. [90] You are just in all your works, holy in all your ways. You are the most wise. All your works from eternity are known to you. You are the most powerful; none can oppose you.

The Lord of hosts is your name, great in counsel and powerful in deeds. Your eyes look down upon all human beings. You are present everywhere; you fill heaven and earth. You are eternal; you see, hear, and rule everything, and sustain it all with the strength of your Word.

You are awesome: when you grant judgment to be proclaimed, the realm of the earth is terrified and stilled. You gain honor upon the earth; you gain honor among the peoples. You wrest courage from the princes, and are to be feared among the kings of the earth. You are to be feared when you are enraged. Who can stand before you when you are angry? The heathen become despondent, and kingdoms fall. When you speak, the kingdom of the earth must fade away.[92]

You are also very gracious, merciful, patient, of great good, and soon regret the punishment you applied. You do not remain angry forever, and you do not remember sins forever. As great as your omnipotence is, just as great is your mercy. Your strength is endless, and your compassion is eternal.

O Eternal Light! O Eternal Salvation! O Eternal Love! O Eternal Sweetness! [91] let me see you, let me experience you, let me taste you. O Eternal Beloved One, O Eternal Comfort, O Eternal Joy! let me rest in you.

In you I find everything I lack in this life of misery. You are full and overflowing, and outside of you is vain poverty, wretchedness, and misery. Life without you is bitter death. Your goodness is better than life.

Oh, most precious Treasure, eternal Good, most beloved Life! When shall I be joined with you in perfect union, that I may see you completely? Holy God, immortal God, righteous God, omniscient God, you who are Eternal King: To you be praise, honor, and glory in all eternity. Amen.

☩

Prayer of a Traveler

Heavenly Father, merciful, faithful God, I thank you wholeheartedly that you have protected me so graciously until now, and have granted me so much goodness for body and soul. I pray, O Lord, be gracious to me, poor sinner, and for the sake of Jesus Christ, forgive me all my misdeeds. Through the strength of your Holy Spirit, make me holy and renew me more and ever more as I grow older. Thus may I improve in my daily living, walk in your paths, [92] and serve you in holiness and righteousness, as is pleasing to you.

Holy Father, lead and direct me further on this journey through the protection of your dear angels, that I may be safe from robbers and murderers, from a poisonous atmosphere and contagious diseases, from conflict and accident.

Grant me, O Lord! nourishment and clothing. Lead me onto the right path upon which I am to walk. Give your blessing to my travel plans, so that everything may turn out to your honor and for the common good, along with my well-being and that of my family. Meanwhile, also keep and protect my whole family and whatever you have bestowed upon me. Grant that we may see each other again in health and with joy.

I especially pray, my God! keep me from all the deceit and malice of the evil enemy and his pawns. Safeguard and strengthen in me the true and saving faith, in repentance, patience, and hope. Grant that I, comforted, may complete the pilgrimage of this impoverished life with uninjured conscience, unto a blessed end. May I joyously enter into the heavenly fatherland.

To you, O Lord! I commend my going out and coming in, from now to eternity, through Jesus Christ. Amen. Our Father . . . [the Lord's Prayer]. [93]

✠

Prayer for Faithful Laborers in the Lord's Harvest

O almighty, merciful God! you so graciously permit the light of your grace to shine upon many hearts, just as it enlightens dark places. In this initial stage of revelation and knowledge of you and your Son, Jesus Christ, we are beginning to recognize our sins and many shortcomings. Our many mistakes, fears, worries, and imperfections are being stirred up by conscience and more and more brought to mind.

Thus, we humbly pray, think of your previous mercy, of your great acts of goodness with which you often saved the Israelites from their enemies. Think of your mighty strength and power with which you continue to save the true Israel according to the Spirit—all those chosen Christian believers—from every error, oppression, fear, and need.[93] You have purchased them as your possession, through the death of your only Son, our Lord Jesus Christ.

Give and send many harvesters, evangelists, apostles, and prophets who are shaped after your heart and will through Christ, in the Holy Spirit. Send those who desire to hold firmly to the sword of the Spirit and to the enlightening word [94] of the pure, healthy teaching of salvation, which creates clarity. Send those who teach and speak the Word of God with integrity, in your presence and in Christ Jesus. Through the earnest service of these leaders, may your shattered Israel thus be gathered more and more in holiness, righteousness, and truth.

We also pray, Lord Jesus Christ! save us from all our shortcomings. Help us that we may truly become children of peace through your peaceable, eternal gospel. Give grace and power to those with hands raised [in prayer], strength to the weak, and steadfastness to the strong, that they may all follow your Word.

Grant that we may totally and solely seek your glory, in which lies the salvation of our souls. Grant also that we may forget everything temporal and earthly that clings to our hearts. In all seriousness may we strive only after what is eternal and heavenly, through and through. Give us this, Jesus Christ, for your name's sake, for you live and reign with God your Father, and the Holy Spirit, true God! now and into everlasting eternity. Amen. [95]

⁜

Prayer from Paul's Epistle for Enlightenment of the Heart

Oh! Lord God, omnipotent, heavenly, gracious Father! give us poor, needy, impoverished people the spirit of wisdom and the revelation of your knowledge. Enlighten the eyes of our understanding. Strengthen us all in faith, and let that faith grow in Jesus Christ.

Grant us a resolute hope in your mercy, in contrast to the shortsightedness of our sinful conscience. Grant us a

well-founded, well-fashioned love for you and for all people, for your sake. We pray that you would strengthen our
poor and weak consciences. Endow us with the living,
actual strength of your equally omnipotent Word in the
Holy Spirit.

May we in turn acknowledge, keep, and confess the
hope of our calling, the richness of the glorious inheritance among your saints, and the immeasurable greatness
of your power in those who have believed in you. We
acknowledge this to be the result of your mighty power
which you worked in Christ when you raised him from
the dead and set him at your right hand in the heavenly
places. He is far above all rule and authority, power and
dominion, and above every name that is named, [96] not
only in this age, but also in the age to come.

O heavenly Father, since we are your possession, to the
praise of your glory, grant us all this in our hearts. Bestow
on us courage and understanding in the Holy Spirit,
through Jesus Christ, your Son and our Lord, through
whom you have promised to give us all things, in accord
with your divine, perfect will. Amen.[94]

✠

Prayer for Unity of Mind
and Understanding in Godly Matters

O eternal, merciful God! you are a God of peace, love,
and unity, not of conflict and division. With this unity
you view the world in your righteous judgment, knowing
it has forsaken you. You alone can establish and maintain
unity in a world which in its own wisdom has fallen away

from you, especially in those things which relate to your divine truth and the salvation of souls. You let the world divide and splinter into pieces, so that with the false wisdom of disunity which can only lead to disgrace, the world might again turn to you, O Lover of unity!

We are poor sinners whom you have graciously endowed [97] with the ability to understand all this. So we pray and implore you through the Holy Spirit to dispel all confusion. Unify what is divided and make it whole. Also give us the means to seek your unique, eternal truth, which leads to divine unity.

Thus may we turn away from every division and become of one mind, will, conscience, spirit, and understanding, aligned according to Jesus Christ, our Lord. May we then praise and glorify you, the heavenly Father of our Lord Jesus Christ, with steadfast unity and with one voice, through the same Jesus Christ, our Lord, in the Holy Spirit. Amen.

☩

Prayer to the Holy Spirit for Help, Comfort, and Support

We are your forsaken and needy children. Inwardly and outwardly we have been subjected to much distress, anxiety, and danger on account of our sins. So we call upon you today, O Holy Spirit of the heavenly Father and our Lord Jesus Christ! Come to us and bring to us from above a bright beam of your divine light. Enter our dark, murky hearts, so that in your light we may see the eternal light and perceive Jesus Christ clearly. [98]

Come, Father of impoverished orphans! gracious Giver of all good gifts! Come, Cleanser of every impure heart! Exercise your ministry in us. Make us holy, and place upon us the work which you, Christ, received from the Father. You have sent out that work among us, who are so very poor, that we may desire you from our hearts.

Comfort and strengthen us, and stand by us in our needs and in every temptation—in facing the sins that dwell within us, as well as the temptations of the world and of the evil spirit.

Purify our beings from all uncleanliness and evil. Reign over our members, eyes, mouth, speech, words, actions, and thoughts, that we may be pleasing to God in everything. Thus may we walk modestly, disciplined, and righteously in this world, and be found to be children of God.

O most beloved Comforter of disconsolate hearts! O worthy Guest of believing souls! O sweet Refreshment and only Sustainer in our weakness! do not depart from us. Along with God the Father and the Son, make an eternal dwelling in us. Strengthen our weak eyes. Wash all that is impure in us. Heal all the wounds in our flesh. Make straight what is lame and crooked. Renew whatever has grown cold in producing goodness. Lead and guide onto the right path whatever has gone astray and become lost. [99]

O most holy Light! illuminate with the brilliance of your grace the inner recesses of the hearts of your faithful, who today are again submitting themselves to your discipline, teaching, and comfort. We are deeply sorry that we ever saddened you or obstructed your works in us.

Now we know from your teaching, however, that nothing in humankind can be good, holy, innocent, and constant without your help, strength, and action.

We also confess our guilt in all of our sins and transgressions—indeed, in everything whereby we have ever resisted your teaching. We confess our sin, whether it be manifest or hidden, and whether it took place in reflection, thoughts, will, words, or deeds. We are so very poor, miserable, and empty, and we are able to do nothing in our own strength.

We take comfort in one thing only, that Jesus Christ, the Son of God, took mercy upon us. For this we declare to him our praise and thanks, with heartfelt hope, that he may never forsake us. We also believe that in the presence of his heavenly Father, he without ceasing is representing us and indeed all who have submitted to him.

Since you, O Holy Spirit! are the Spirit of the Lord Christ, permit us to enjoy such faithfulness, love, and graciousness. Pour your mighty strength into us. Grant a new, reborn heart to those of us who are weak in [100] faith yet who now are submitting to your discipline in word and heart.

Place in our hearts your holy, sevenfold gifts: the gift of divine wisdom; the gift of a true and new understanding of the Word and will of God; the gift of counsel, unto the praise of his glory; the gift of inner power and strength; the gift of the true knowledge of God and Christ; the gift of the fear of the Lord; and the gift of every blessing.[95]

To us who are poor and forsaken, extend such gracious gifts for the sake of your unspeakable love and goodness, yes, for the sake of the one who has redeemed us with his precious blood.[96] Oh, come to us soon from heaven; do not delay! God the Holy Spirit! do not look upon our manifold sins, since we want to be free and clear of them. So remove them from us, more and more, and have mercy on us.

Take our hearts captive with your precious power, and fill them with heavenly comfort and joy. May we at all times take full comfort in God, being joyful and satisfied in every concern. Thus may we as children of God overcome this evil and wicked world. Praise be to you, O Holy Spirit, with God the Father and the Son, in eternity! Amen. [101]

✠

In Remembrance of Certain Things for Which We Should Sigh and Pray to God

1. That God the Lord would save all discouraged consciences, and all impoverished, anxious, imprisoned persons from distress, and would comfort us and them.

2. That God, through the light of his grace, would discover and reveal every mistake, both old and new, along with every pretense.

3. That God would reveal more and more the true righteousness of the heart, and his holy gospel—through divine strength, in the Holy Spirit, and with conscientious human response.

4. That for this to happen, God would await and bring forth many devout and faithful servants, who are aligned

with his heart, cultivate the conscience, and gather his people in the Holy Spirit.

5. That God would destroy all of the counsel and actions of those who oppose his holy ways, and their decrees which interfere with the true knowledge of God and Christ, snuff out human spirits, grieve the Holy Spirit, and hinder the process of true repentance and salvation.

6. That God would awaken in us desire and love, indeed, also [102] a hunger and thirst for his divine knowledge and will.

7. That we will be serious and steadfast in putting off the old person and putting on the new.

8. That God the Lord would send from heaven his Holy Spirit, for the sake of Christ, to lead us into all truth; that we through the Spirit may reach the goal of being one heart, one soul, one in spirit, one mind, and become wholly and truly one in Christ Jesus.

9. That in our teaching and life, in our walk and being, we may always look upon the one Master, Christ Jesus; that we may have God before our eyes constantly, walking always in his fear, and learning to use all things well.

10. For all our brothers and sisters, who patiently remain steadfast with us in the one true faith, one hope, one love of God, and one Lord Christ—that all of us may obtain comfort, peace, and joy in our hearts. Amen.

✠
Manasseh the King's Prayer
[for Forgiveness]

I have sinned, and my sin is greater than the sands of the sea.[97] I am bound in iron fetters and have no peace. With my sin, O God! I have awakened your wrath, and [103] I have committed great evil before you. Since I have caused so much abomination and wickedness, I bend the knees of my heart[98] and ask you, Lord! for grace.

O Lord! I have sinned. Indeed, I have sinned, and I confess my transgression. So now I pray and solemnly implore you, forgive me for this, O Lord! Forgive me for this, and do not let me perish in my sins. Do not let the punishment remain upon me forever. May you help me in accord with your great mercy. I in turn want to praise you at all times as long as I live. [Amen.]

✠
The Prayer of Daniel,
in Chapter Nine

O Lord! great and terrible God, you hold to your covenant and mercy for those who love you and keep your commandments. We have sinned; we have erred; we have been ungodly and have fallen away. Indeed, we have departed from all your commands and judgments.

We have never even desired to follow the prophets, your servants, who spoke in your name to our kings and princes, our ancestors, and to all the people of the land. Therefore, the Lord has sent this calamity upon us. For the Lord our God is righteous in all his works. Yet we do not want [104] to follow his voice.

O Lord, our God, with a mighty hand you led your people out of Egypt. Thereby you created for yourself a name which remains even to this day. We have sinned and acted in an ungodly manner against all your righteousness. For on account of our sins and the misdeeds of our fathers, Jerusalem and your people have been scorned by everyone living round about us.

However, O Lord! desist from your terrible wrath over the city of Jerusalem and your holy mountain. Hear the prayer of your servant, and let your face shine over your holy place. Oh, my God, bend your ear and listen. Open your eyes and look at our desolation and the city which is called by your name.

Oh, Lord! hear us; oh, Lord! forgive us; oh, Lord! take note of our prayer. For we are not praying on the grounds of our piety, but rather on the grounds of your great mercy. Help us, and do not delay. [Amen.][99]

⚜

Prayer of a Sad and Depressed Person

Oh, dear Lord and God! I, miserable and weak, come to you and ask from my heart that you might listen to me in my distress. For you indeed have promised in your Word, rich in love, that you desire to listen to the sorrowful.

Oh, dear Father! [105] listen to me for the sake of Jesus Christ, for the anxiety of my heart is great. O Lord! listen to me in my great anguish, for you have, O Lord! saved everyone who has called on you with their whole heart.

I call to you humbly in Jesus' name. Come to me with help, for I am desperate. Otherwise, I shall perish. O God! The waves of affliction slam against my little ship; it seems about to sink. So from the depths of my soul, I call to you, O God! with genuine grief, just as Jairus called to you for his little daughter.[100] Oh, come to me with help before I sink in my deep depression.

O dear Father! do not be angry over my timid heart. I pray along with the centurion: I confess that I am not worthy for you to come into my house, since it is full of sin and without love and understanding.[101]

Oh, God! not only that. Oh! I have spent the recent past completely avoiding the fear of God. Oh! I am sorry that I have so lived, for you know everything through and through. I have had more earthly than heavenly joy; for that, you have let me experience much horror, anxiety, and dejection. I never would have thought or believed that such despondent thoughts could attack me.

Oh, Lord! Your servant, David, also suffered such affliction [106] when he said, The anxiety of my heart is great.[102] He also called out in great distress, his heart shuddering with fear that he would never again be joyous. Oh, dear Father! look upon me: this too has happened within me.

Thoughts often come to me that there may be no more hope to be drawn from the well. Oh, how often have the words come to me: Distress has completely surrounded me; misery has flattened me.[103] Oh, dear Father! I am terrified that the same will happen to me. Yet I know that you know everything far better than I could ever explain it to you.

Therefore, I pray even more, have mercy on me. Console me, O Lord! in my distress. Since you are so merciful, I pray with Mary Magdalene: Oh, Lord! see, like that impure woman, I am sorely afraid and in need of help. And I ask, help me, weak as I am. If I could only touch the hem of your garment, I would be made whole.[104]

Oh, dear Lord! Strengthen me, weak person that I am, as you strengthened your servant who also suffered such anxiety, saying, Let my grace be sufficient for you.[105] But alas, I cannot get ahold of myself, since my inner fear is so great, and my thoughts terrify me.

Indeed, I confess I am so depressed that I can say with David, I wither like grass.[106] Yes, if you, O Father-Heart, do not again refresh me, [107], my salvation will fade. Nothing more is in me that can revive me, except for the one thing which you alone can do. Indeed, I must say, I am wasting away like an evening shadow.

Yet you can again make me rejoice if you so desire, for your miracles are abundant. Oh Lord! I call with Jonah from the depths of my despondent heart. I shout to you with that blind person, Have mercy on me, O Jesus, Son of David! If you so desire, you can certainly help me.[107]

O Lord! I certainly have often been disobedient to your fatherly voice. I confess this with a humble heart and come to you as a child to his father, saying, How deeply fearful I am, because of my great sin. I have sinned and done evil before you, O Father!

Oh! look upon me graciously, I pray from the depths of my heart, and save me from my temptation.[108] Oh, Father! pour out your mercy upon me and comfort me again with your fatherly help. With David, I call to you from my heart, O dear God and Father! Create in me a pure heart, O God! and give me a new and right Spirit,[109] that henceforth I may serve you in love, in trust, in safety, and in childlike hope, humbly and with my whole heart.

Oh! with your holy and good Spirit, make me secure in my heart, [108] mind, and thoughts, in my faith, love, and hope. Thus may I remain truly steadfast in you, and finally die, confident of being blessed and of rising again joyously. All this I pray in the name of Jesus Christ, O dear, merciful Father and Holy Spirit! triune Being in eternity, unto the praise, honor, and glory of your holy name. Amen, Amen, in the name of Jesus our Savior, Amen.

☦

A Prayer Before the Sermon
To Be Offered with a Devout Heart

O Lord, almighty God! dear holy and heavenly Father! You are our Creator, Redeemer, Preserver, and Provider.[110] You provide us not only with all kinds of temporal necessities; you also give us the true living bread from heaven, with which you feed our souls for eternal life.

We poor children do not live by bread alone, but by every word that proceeds from your mouth,[111] according to the testimony of your beloved Son, Jesus Christ. In his name we now are assembled here in your presence, to proclaim, to hear, [109] and to understand what is your holy and divine will for us. You, O God! have kindled in us this zeal and have put into our hearts this desire and love for this work. Thus we have gladly and freely gathered for that purpose, coming together in a spirit of unity. We thank and praise you for all this from the depth of our hearts.

However, dear merciful Father! with our human limitations, we are not worthy, skilled, or able to proclaim your divine Word, to hear it, much less to keep it, without your divine, gracious aid and the participation of your good Holy Spirit. We therefore beseech you, dear Father! open your eyes of mercy upon us at this time, that the promise of your beloved Son may be fulfilled in us.

O Christ! be in the midst of this congregation with the power and grace of your Holy Spirit. Make your servant competent, and put holy words into his mouth. Grant him openness and courage to speak out with true discernment according to your holy and divine will, and then bless and consecrate what you have given him.

Open as well the ears of our hearts, and give us obedient hearts, [110] cleansed of every vain thought and passing concern. So may we hear your divine Word, understand it, and faithfully keep it in faith and obedience.

O God! may this be done to the praise, honor, and glory of your holy, praiseworthy, and glorious name. For all people everywhere may it be an admonition to obedience. And for all of us gathered here, may it confirm eternal salvation. This we ask, O God, through Jesus Christ, your Son, our Lord and Savior, who taught us reverently to pray: Our Father . . . [the Lord's Prayer].

✠
Another Worshipful, General Prayer
For Attaining the Ability to Pray, the Forgiveness of Sins,
the Cleansing of Life, Divine Enlightenment, and the
Revelation of the Countenance of God

Just as we, O heavenly Father! have committed ourselves to calling upon your holy name, so also look upon
us with the eyes of your mercy.[112] Incline your ears, open
your generous hand, and give us cleansed, obedient hearts,
that we may lift them up to you, O God and Father in
heaven!

There at your right hand we have our Redeemer and
[111] Savior, Jesus Christ, your beloved Son. For our jus-
tification he ascended into heaven, where we cannot yet
follow him bodily as long as we inhabit this dwelling.[113]
But he has comforted us and given us the firm promise
that what we ask of you in his name, O Father! you will
grant and give us.[114]

We acknowledge our powerlessness and nothingness.
So we come before you, dear Father, and pray that you
will give us a steadfast and firm confidence in our hearts,
so we may be able to hear, examine, and comprehend
your truth. May you keep us firm and immovable, as you
have promised through your Son.

O Lord! seal this truth in our hearts. Yes, dear Father!
strengthen our confidence to enable us to fathom how
deeply you love the human race, to which you are so
inclined and willing to give every good gift. May we firmly trust your almighty power, for we know that you, O
God! make no promises that you cannot abundantly ful-

fill. Since you desire our well-being even more than we ourselves do, grant us not to look upon our unworthiness, [112] but only upon your kindness, goodness, truth, and unlimited power.

Because we ought to call upon you with confidence, O God and Father! free our hearts of vain and deadly thoughts and desires so that no unrighteousness will be found in them. May we ask or desire only what is pleasing to you, O God! to your praise, and for the salvation of our souls.

To that end, make our hearts lowly and humble, so that our prayers do not come back to us empty, but that they may pierce through the clouds to you, O God and Father! Grant us also a heart that willingly forgives our neighbor without nursing any desire for revenge. Break, strike, and crush our hearts until they shed a flood of tears which you, O Father! can consider and which will be pleasing to you.

We also ask you to give us a deep desire and inclination of heart, and a sweet, reverent nature to call upon you as our Father, O God! with childlike love. We address you in the name of your beloved Son, Jesus Christ, whose power is strong and mighty. You love him so dearly that you cannot refuse what we pray in his name. [113] He removes from us, O God! whatever is displeasing to you. He prepares life and grace for us. He is our intercessor and prays for us.

We therefore ask you in his name for the remission and pardon of our sins. Lord! forgive us our sins in the name of your dear Son, Jesus Christ.

You are our God and Creator, who has given us breath

and life. So direct the ordering of our life for eternal salvation. For all our works, deeds, and undertakings are in your hands. O Lord! direct them according to your divine pleasure; we commit them into your mighty hand.

However, O God, like the earth without rain and dew, we too are unfruitful without your favor and grace and must perish and dry up. Shower and moisten us with your heavenly dew, rain, and favor; prepare us to bear fruit. This we also ask, dear Father! in Jesus' name.

You alone are wise. Not only do you live in the light, but you yourself are the eternal light. We are living here in this dark, blind world; so enlighten us, O God! with your [114] divine wisdom, which is a co-worker of your throne. Send down your wisdom from your holy heaven and the throne of your glory, to be with us and work with us, so we may know what is pleasing to you. Without this gift, O God! we cannot please you. For this wisdom, Lord! we also ask in the name of your beloved Son, Jesus Christ, in whom are hidden all the riches of wisdom and knowledge.[115]

Since we now are burdened with all kinds of anxieties, we pray to you with David: O Lord! show us your countenance, and we shall be made well, that we may look upon it and live.[116] For therein rests our salvation and eternal life. All the saints and your elect possess and enjoy that goodness. Let us also enjoy and share in this, in the name of Jesus Christ, your Son, who taught us to pray. Grant that we may speak in spirit and truth as we say, Our Father . . . [the Lord's Prayer].

✠

Another Short Prayer
After the Sermon

O gracious, merciful God! dear heavenly Father! you show and prove to us, your poor children, your abundant goodness and love.[117] [115] You have not only given us this desire, zeal, and willing spirit to assemble here before you in your holy name. You have also allowed us to hear your Word (as has happened often and frequently before this), and thereby your divine will has been presented and proclaimed.

For granting us this favor, O Lord! we thank and praise you from the bottom of our hearts and from the depth of our souls. We willingly confess our guilt because we so often have been admonished and have heard your faithful warning, but have not hastened to obey. O Lord! forgive us for the sake of your beloved Son, Jesus Christ.

Now that we have heard and received your Word, we also beseech you, dear merciful Father! to make it alive, powerful, and effective in all our hearts, and cause it to bear fruit that will remain unto life eternal. We ask that we may not only be reborn, thoroughly transformed, changed, and renewed completely in your likeness. May we also be brought thereby to the perfect stature of Christ and thus grow, increase, and be sustained.[118]

Yes, grant that we may set your Word as a mirror before the eyes [116] of our heart, and use it as living water to wash ourselves. Grant that we may thereby become cleansed and pure, that the fruits of righteousness may spring from your Word, and we may become equipped and prepared for every good work. May our poor souls also be made alive and well, till your Word thus penetrates our hearts, separating soul and spirit, joint and marrow.[119]

Grant that your Word will bring us to be not earthly but heavenly minded, that it may ignite us and make us fervent and aflame to produce all virtues. May we thereby become utterly humbled and lowly of heart, wholly renewed, moved to weep with others, to suffer with others, and to show compassion.

Let us also taste the sweetness of your divine grace and of the eternal heavenly kingdom, taking our delight in it alone.

Finally, may we attain victory over the sly attacks of the devil and all the weapons of the enemy, and be kept eternally safe.

Thus we ask you, dear Father! for all of our necessities (etc.), all this through your dearly beloved Son, our Lord Jesus Christ, who taught us, for attaining your divine grace, to pray: Our Father . . . [the Lord's Prayer]. [117]

✠

A Brief Prayer for Use with Holy Baptism

O almighty God and dear merciful Father! you knew from eternity that the humanity you created would not remain in its innocent state but would experience a Fall.[120] Not only that, but you knew the human race would load upon itself the just blame for its punishment. You (who love your creation) have also from eternity provided for humanity in the fullness of time.[121]

You did not spare your only Son, but sent and gave

him up for all humanity, so that all who believe in him should not perish but have everlasting life.[122] You proclaimed and offered such love and grace to humanity through your holy gospel. By this same message you commanded that all who accept and believe the gospel are to submit to baptism in the name of Jesus.

Through your grace this has been taken to heart by those present. They now are sitting before you with bowed knees of the heart,[123] confessing that they are ready to perform your divine will and the command of your beloved Son.

They reject the devil, the world, and their own flesh and blood.[124] They desire to live only for Jesus Christ, who died for them, arose, [118] and went to heaven. They confess him to be the Son of the living God, their Savior and Redeemer. They willingly consent to place their faith in your holy gospel, and they give themselves in complete obedience to it.

However, dear gracious Father! you know that obedience is beyond human power; by ourselves, we cannot obey. You are the one, O God! who through grace must accomplish in us the will and the deeds. So now, dear Lord! turn the eyes of your mercy upon these your creatures, your creation.

Lay your almighty hand upon this work, so that these persons may be able, by your power, to strive and conquer sin, the world, the devil, and hell, that they may be crowned as heavenly kings.

May they, having rejected all love for the world, be washed beautiful and clean, as a pure virgin to be presented as a bride to Christ, your Son.[125] May they forsake

the kingdom of the devil, which is sin, and become joint
heirs of your heavenly kingdom of righteousness.[126] May
they, through the covenant which they are now making
with you unto obedience, have a good conscience regard-
ing the forgiveness of their sins. [119] May their hope for
eternal life be joyous.

Heavenly Father! accept them in your mercy, forgive
their sins, elect them to be your children, and through
grace make them joint heirs of your heavenly possessions.

O Christ! Son of God! endow them with all your merits, and share with them all your goodness and righteousness. Wash them in your blood. Accept them as your
brothers and sisters and as joint heirs of your heavenly
kingdom.

O gracious Holy Spirit! impart your gifts to them,
establish them in the faith, kindle prayer in them, and
begin their renewal, that they may put fleshly deeds to
death[127] and follow your call. Keep and preserve them in
the faith, that they may overcome doubt and death. Do
all this to the honor and praise of your divine glory and
for the salvation of their souls. For this we now beseech
you with one mind, saying, Our Father . . . [the Lord's
Prayer].

In your name, O God! shall this work be begun; complete it through the power of your divine grace. This we
ask through your Son, Jesus Christ. Amen. [120]

⊹

A Short Unison Prayer

To Be Offered with Reverent Hearts by the Assembled
Believers Observing the Holy Supper of the Lord

O Lord! almighty, merciful God and dear Father! at this time we are assembled in your presence to keep the blessed memorial of the broken body and shed blood of your Son, Jesus Christ, and to enjoy this blessed communion.[128]

O dear heavenly Father! make all of us together worthy and fit to sit at this table as spiritual, invited friends. May we be reminded of all the mystery of this meal, so that we may partake of it profitably, to your honor and for our salvation.

We also sincerely and willingly confess our sins, our unworthiness and nothingness. We come before you stripped of all righteousness, and seek to console ourselves with the righteousness which Christ, your Son, obtained for us with his bitter death, suffering, and shed blood.

O Lord! through your grace and the gift of the Holy Spirit, grant that our hungering souls may in this meal be fed with the body and blood of your beloved Son. May he remain in us and we in him, so [121] that his bitter suffering for us may not have been in vain. May our hope be strengthened thereby, and may we have the assurance in our hearts that through the breaking of the bread, we are partakers in all his suffering and merits.

May we also be assured thereby of your most gracious and steadfast covenant that you, O God, will be our gracious Provider and Protector. May we, thus assured and strengthened, show true gratitude from the depth of our souls.

May we henceforth continue to grow and increase in faith, in love, in patience, in the willingness to bear your Son's cross, and in all the Christian virtues. And may we, with a renewed, temperate, righteous, and devout life, serve you for the rest of our lives. Thus may your holy name be honored, and may we dwell eternally with you through Christ. Amen. Our Father . . . [the Lord's Prayer].

☩
Thanksgiving with the Breaking of the Bread

℧ Lord, almighty God! dear heavenly Father! you have loved us.[129] In order to redeem us from eternal death, you have given your dear Son, Jesus Christ, as our reconciliation [122], that our souls may be fed by this heavenly Bread for eternal life. In pure grace you have called us poor souls to this holy communion. For this, we offer praise and thanks, blessing and honor, and everlasting glory, through your Son, Jesus Christ, our Lord and Savior. Amen.

☩
Thanksgiving with the Sharing of the Cup

℧ Lord, almighty God! dear heavenly Father! you have led out your people through the ministry of the only great Shepherd of your sheep, Jesus Christ, through the blood of the eternal covenant, that he shed for us on the cross for our reconciliation.[130] You have called us by grace to this blessed communion. For this we give you praise and thanks, blessing and honor and everlasting glory, through your Son, the same Jesus Christ, our Lord. Amen. [123]

✠

A Short Prayer for Those About to Be Married
To Be Spoken with a Reverent Heart

O Lord, almighty, merciful God! in your eternal wisdom and goodness you have seen that it is not good for man, created in your image, to be alone.[131] Hence, in the beginning you gave him a helper (the woman, made from his rib) for the propagation of the human race. To avoid impurity, you also instituted holy matrimony, which your beloved Child, Jesus Christ, reformed and confirmed.[132]

Thus, O God, these two now stand before you, ready to enter into such a marriage and to establish it in conformity with your divine will.

Turn the eyes of your mercy upon them, and bless and consecrate them, O God. Grant them your divine grace, that their hearts, spirits, and intentions may be set on you alone, to seek solely your divine honor and the salvation of their souls. May they in this way, as is fitting for the saints, establish and keep this marriage and be protected from the temptations of the devil. Whatever by way of cross, suffering, and future distress [124] might befall them, may they during these times experience your divine comfort.

We ask this for them, O God and Father! through your dearly beloved Son, Jesus Christ our Lord, who taught us in all our needs and concerns to pray: Our Father . . . [the Lord's Prayer].

⛭

Yet Another Short Morning Prayer

Lord God! dear heavenly Father! you are our Creator and Provider, under whose gracious protection and care we rested well again last night.[133] For this we praise and thank you.

However, O dear Father! whatever misuse we may meanwhile have made of your benevolence, in any way contrary to your divine will, we readily confess with remorse. Forgive us for the sake of Christ, your dear Son.

Teach us to reflect on why you have let this new day dawn, so we may spend it and all the coming days of our lives soberly, righteously, and devoutly. Thus may your holy name be honored and praised, and may we be graciously kept and blessed forever.

To this end may your good Spirit guide us, and may your good angels make our path joyous. [125] This we pray, O God, in the name of your beloved Son, Jesus Christ, who taught us to pray: Our Father . . . [the Lord's Prayer].

⚜

Another Short Evening Prayer

O dear merciful heavenly Father! you have permitted us to enjoy the clear light of the sun today, that we may walk uprightly according to your divine will.[134] Hence, we thank your holy name for this and ask you to forgive us for neglecting to do what we should have done, and for acting against your will. This we freely confess.

Grant us your grace that we may lie down to rest under the shadow of your wings of divine mercy. May we be protected and preserved against all the treacherous onslaughts of the enemy, who moves around us by day and by night. Thus may we use the night's rest gratefully. May we be constantly mindful of the coming of your beloved Son, through whom we pour out from our hearts the following prayer to you: Our Father . . . [the Lord's Prayer]. [126]

⚜

Prayer Before the Meal

The eyes of all believers are turned in hope to you, O Lord God, dear heavenly Father! and await your divine support for their welfare.[135] At the proper time you give them their spiritual and natural food (as you do for all your creatures).

Since you are the Provider of all, you open your kind hand and pour out your goodness and blessing upon those whose hope is in you, whose eyes look up to you. So help us, Lord! to turn the eyes of our hearts to you in trust. Thus may we too enjoy the blessing and benediction of your gracious divine gifts, partake of these, your gifts, in moderation, and use them to your glory and for our needs.

Above all, may our souls be fed constantly with the bread of your divine Word unto eternal life, through your dear Son, Jesus Christ, our Lord. Amen.

✠

Prayer and Thanksgiving After the Meal

O Lord! dear heavenly Father! we have now received these gifts from your kind hand.[136] [127] We have enjoyed them and satisfied our hunger with them. These gifts, like all the other gifts, you bestow upon us so lavishly that we should love you from our hearts and glorify you with the tongue.

We ask through Christ your Son that you would fill us through the power of your Holy Spirit in us. May we who are receiving these gifts from you not become proud and haughty, or forgetful of your love and your holy commandments. Instead, may we love you with our whole heart, love you not only with our mouth and lips, but also with all our works and deeds and all that is in us.

Thus may we thank, praise, honor, and glorify you, as our Creator and Preserver, not only in this life but also in the imperishable eternal life. In your honor we now pray, saying, Our Father . . . [the Lord's Prayer].

✠
Prayer for and with the Sick

Lord, almighty God! you have created human beings in your image.[137] In your eternal wisdom and kindness, you love them all and provide them with all that is necessary for eternal life.

You know that it benefits people [128] to be disciplined for their transformation. Hence, you afflict and burden them with different sorts of sickness and weakness, so that their pride and futile confidence may be subdued, lest they be completely ruined.

You admonish them thereby to forsake their sinful lives, to consider their end. Through pain and sorrow you make them mindful of death, since those aches are forerunners of their end. You remind them of your stern and righteous judgment on judgment day, and of eternal life. You make them mindful of these things, not in wrath, but in fatherly chastisement.

Dear merciful Father! you have now visited and laid ___ (this person here)[138] low with sickness and suffering for correction, under your almighty hand. The frailty of imperfect human life may be accusing ___, and death often stares such a one in the face.[139] We therefore pray to you humbly, with ___ and beside ___.

O dear merciful Father! through the shed blood of your beloved Son, our Lord Jesus Christ, we ask you not to deal with ___ in accord with the severity of your just judgment and what ___ may deserve, but in accord with your mercy and kindness. Grant ___ inner comfort and strength to accept your fatherly visitation willingly, [129] to bear it patiently, and during this affliction to remain obedient to you, O God!

Stand by ___, dear Father! in every conflict, and protect ___ in all the anxiety and danger facing ___. Especially, O God! if ___ is to uncover and reveal to you
the knowledge of ___ heart, help ___ to admit and confess that ___ is sinful and guilty before you, and forgive
___.

In kindness and grace, pour out over ___ the benefits
of the severe, bitter suffering of your beloved Son, Christ,
who has in truth borne our sickness and taken upon him-
self our punishment when he became sin for us.[140] He died
for our sins, shedding his precious blood to wash them
away.[141] He rose from the dead to become our righteousness and perfect Savior.[142]

O God! graciously permit this poor, sick person to
enjoy abundantly all of these immeasurably great gifts of
grace, and the manifold kind deeds of your dear Son.

O Lord! strengthen ___ in genuine faith. Serve as a secure comfort against the ravages of sin, as a shield against
all the treacherous attacks of the devil. Thus may ___
[130] pass through death to life, and after this short, fleeting life, attain everlasting life and be preserved for eternal health.

O heavenly Father! we commend ___ completely into
your hands. O true Savior, return this patient to health.
O true Helper in times of trial! help this weak person.
Raise ___ up! from ___ dejection of heart. Wash ___,
who is confessing ___ uncleanness. Bind ___ wounds, for
___ is miserably wounded. O God, strengthen this weak
person, laden with fear.

Because you can do all things abundantly, satisfy this

hungering and thirsting one with heavenly food. As ___ turns to you, accept ___ graciously. Make ___ steadfast in ___ good intentions, according to your will.

Forgive ___ everything that has earned your wrath and anger, and instead of death, give ___ eternal life. Grant all this out of grace, through Jesus Christ, your Son, our Lord, who for the comfort of all penitent sinners and as an example to them, also took the evildoer on the cross with him into paradise.[143] He lives and reigns with you in the unity of the Holy Spirit, true God unto eternity. Amen. [131]

☩

A Sick Person's Prayer of Comfort

Oh, Lord, merciful, holy, and righteous God! I confess to you that with my innumerable sins, I have provoked your just anger. You are just, and your judgments are also just. Oh! how with all my heart I regret that I have so often and so deeply grieved you, my most beloved Father. I have been so ungrateful for your great deeds of kindness. Oh, Lord! do not be angry nor remember forever the sins of my youth, or my transgressions. Instead, remember all these things according to your mercy, on account of your goodness.

Oh, Lord! this is certainly your just punishment, which is fair for me to bear, for I have sinned against you. However, I turn in faith to face the only throne of grace,[144] to my Lord Jesus Christ. I bend the knees of my heart[145] before you and pray for grace and forgiveness.

O Lord! may I find grace and attain mercy. Have mercy on me, and take this affliction from me. Oh, Lord!

my sins have poisoned me, and my misdeeds have led to this evil illness[146] which has laid me so low. Oh, Lord! you who heal everything through your Word, forgive. Forgive me, and heal [132] me of this scourge. Oh, Lord! you heal all those who call upon you in faith. I am looking upon the crucified Jesus with eyes of faith; let my soul recover.

O Lord! my perishable body is full of sins. Therefore, it is also full of sickness and pain. Bestow your mercy upon me, a poor Lazarus lying before your door, full of sickness and pain. I want to be filled with your bread of grace. Oh, Lord, Lord! look upon your dear Son, who bore my sickness and was wounded on account of my sins.[147] You provide, dear Father, my desire for life. You are indeed my light and salvation and the strength of my life. Do not permit me to perish in this illness.

Keep me, Lord! under your almighty umbrella of protection and under the shadow of your wings of grace. Mark me with the blood of Jesus Christ, the Lamb without blemish, that the angel of death may pass over me.[148]

Strengthen me, Lord! with your Spirit and your power, and give me a strong, firm faith that I may speak to you. My Refuge and my God, in whom I hope, save me! May your wisdom be my protection. May I not be frightened on account of this affliction. Command your angel to protect me at all times. [133]

O Lord! help me, for I desire your help. O Lord! I confess your name; therefore protect me. O Lord! I call to you; therefore hear me. O Lord! remain with me in my time of need. Deliver me from my plight with your almighty hand, and show me your eternal salvation in Jesus Christ, our dear Savior. Amen.

☦

A Funeral Prayer

ᗴear Lord God, merciful, heavenly Father, we thank you that you have not created us only for this earthly life, but also, already from eternity and in accord with your immeasurable grace, have chosen us to partake of heavenly and eternal life. You have won and prepared us for eternal life through your dear Son, Jesus Christ.

Therefore, we now have this secure comfort that when we have completed the walk of our life according to your divine Word and will, we shall enter your heavenly Jerusalem. There, at your right hand, we shall have fullness of joy and delightful existence, forever.

O dear Father! we thank you also for all your deeds of kindness which you have bestowed upon ___ (the deceased person).[149] We thank you especially that you have saved ___ from the misery of this sinful world, [134] have brought an end to ___ sorrow, and as we hope, have granted ___ a blessed end.

Oh, Lord! we pray that you may also provide for all of us assembled here a blessed end, and a joyous resurrection on the last day, the day of judgment. It is established that all of us will die some day, after which comes the judgment.[150] Therefore, teach us so to number our days that we may gain wisdom in our hearts.[151] May we fear you as our God and during the short time of our life, turn ourselves to your service, so we will not be unprepared and slip out of your hand.

Increase in us, O Lord! that faith in the Lord Jesus Christ which alone brings salvation, so we can take comfort in his precious merit in life and in death. Grant that we may devote ourselves constantly to being devout, humble, and loving, and in serving others in need.

Protect us from a consuming love for this world, and from what is attached to the world: from pride, impatience, anger, and from everything which contradicts sound teaching. Strengthen us through the power of your Holy Spirit, so that we can vigorously oppose the devil, the world, and our tainted flesh, [135] and defeat and overcome all these, our enemies.

Grant us grace to live here on earth in such a way that we are prepared daily, indeed hourly, to depart from here in peace, and to enter into your heavenly joy.

Strengthen us, and comfort also all who are sick and sorrowful of heart. Be gracious to them, and give them to know that you are disciplining them out of love.

Especially, however, may you comfort mightily those who are saddened now by the departure of ___, our dear (brother/sister) in the faith. Help them graciously to enter once again into joy, through an unexpected blessing in their sorrow.

O Lord! since you are our God and Creator, who has given us breath and life, align our life's pattern to that of eternal salvation. All our works, our actions, and activities lie in your hands. O Lord! direct them by your divine will and pleasure. We commend them to your mighty care.

Yet, O God! just as the earth without rain and dew remains barren, so also we without your grace and favor can only dry up and perish. Therefore, shower us with your [136] heavenly dew, rain, and favor, and prepare us to bear fruit. We pray all this, O dear Father! in the name of your dear Son, Jesus Christ.

Oh, holy Father! we also pray for our children, indeed, for all children, all those for whom you desire our prayers. Give them wisdom and understanding in their hearts. May they acknowledge your Word and your will with their whole heart. With the discipline of your mercy, nurture them unto the knowledge of your eternal truth.

Since you are the eternal light and they are living in this dark and deluded world, enlighten them with your divine wisdom. Bless them with your Holy Spirit, guard them against every idolatry and false teaching, and plant in them the unique saving faith in the Lord Jesus Christ.

O Lord! send down your holy angels from above to keep our children safe on all their paths, so that they may offer a mighty resistance to the devil, the world, and their own flesh.

We pray, O holy Father! do not allow the number of unrighteous to increase through us or our children. Instead, give us much more grace that we may raise our children in the true Christian virtues, disciplining them without [137] bitter zeal or anger. Indeed, may we lead them as good models in our teaching, life, and walk, so that they may be built up and strengthened through our life and conduct. Thereby may the number of your holy, chosen children increase through us and our children.

We pray, O dear Father! for widows and orphans, and for all who are troubled and despondent. Give them as much grace and patience as they need to remain steadfast until their blessed end.

O Lord! have mercy upon all our enemies and all who hate you and us, those who continue to live unconcerned for the salvation of their souls. Let them know how deeply they have sinned against you, so they may be alarmed, mend their ways, and repent. Thus may their souls be saved.

Finally, O Lord, when our hour of death approaches, undergird us all with your strength. Help us to fight a good fight and finish the course. Thus may we also obtain the crown of righteousness which you have promised to all those who love the appearing of your Son.[152] Into your hands, O Lord, faithful God! we commend our souls,[153] for you have saved us through Jesus Christ. Amen. [138]

Grant that we may be able to say, in spirit and in truth, Our Father . . . [the Lord's Prayer].

✠

Prayer for Maintaining the Christian Faith and Christian Virtues Until Our Blessed End

O Lord, heavenly Father! from whom come all good and perfect gifts. Father of Light! you who work in us both to will and to do for your good pleasure.[154] O Lord Jesus Christ! you who are the pioneer and perfecter of our faith.[155] And O Holy Spirit! you who work all in all according to your good pleasure.[156]

We entreat you from our hearts that you would bring to completion the good work which you have begun in us, until the day of Jesus Christ. Thus may we more and more become rich in every type of knowledge and experience, that we might determine what is the best. So may we remain pure and blameless until the day of Jesus

Christ, filled with the harvest of righteousness produced in us through Jesus Christ, for the glory of God.[157] [139]

Oh, God! we are carrying a treasure in earthly vessels,[158] but the devil, the world, and our own flesh torment us and battle against the soul. Grant that we may fight valiantly and win the victory. May we overcome these enemies in us and give our bodies as a sacrifice which is holy, living, and pleasing to God. May we be transformed through the renewing of our minds, so that we might prove what is the good, gracious, acceptable, and perfect will of God.[159]

Grant us strength, O Lord Jesus! to strive for the richness of your glory. Through your Spirit may we become strong in our inner being. Grant that through faith you might dwell in our hearts, and that we might be rooted and grounded in love. Thus may we learn to know how high and how deep your love is, and learn to have love for Christ and to become filled with every sort of God's fullness, which is better than all knowledge.[160]

Oh, dear heavenly Father! it is indeed your will that you shall lose no one from all those whom you have given to your dear Son. Therefore, keep us in the faith, fortify us in love, strengthen us in hope.

Oh, holy Trinity! come and dwell with us. Fill us here [on earth] with [140] your grace, and there [in heaven] with your eternal splendor. Hear our prayer. Give us your Holy Spirit, to enlighten us with your divine Word, to make us holy, and to teach, strengthen, ground, and keep us unto eternal life.

Send your light and your truth to lead us and take us to your dwelling place. May we fight a good fight. May we hold to the faith and to a good conscience. Lead us in your truth and teach us, for you are the God who helps us. Day by day we trust confidently in you.[161]

Be mindful, Lord, of your mercy and your goodness, which has existed from the beginning of the world. Do not remember the sins of our youthful years, nor our transgressions. Be mindful of us in accord with your mercy, for the sake of your goodness.

Oh, Lord Jesus! grant us true repentance, heartfelt remorse and sorrow for our sins, a godly sadness working in us a regret that no one regrets having. Thus may our hearts be prepared, opening to your comfort and your most worthy forgiveness of sin. Grant us the spirit of love, of gentleness, of humility, of worship, of divine fear, of grace, and of prayer. Thus may we with all saints possess [141] your kingdom and grasp your love and eternal life.

O God! enlighten us with your Holy and good Spirit. Turn our hearts from the world, from the lust of the eyes, the lust of the flesh, and the pride of life.[162] Grant that we may truly sanctify the holy and most praiseworthy name of God, glorifying it at all times. May we no longer blaspheme that name or deny it during times of persecution, but confess it even in the throes of death.

Grant that God's kingdom may be in us and remain in us, and that the devil's kingdom might be destroyed. Safeguard us from lies and deception, from blindness and darkness of heart. Create in us righteousness, peace, and joy in the Holy Spirit.[163] And may the peace of God, which surpasses all understanding, keep our hearts and minds in Christ Jesus, our Lord.[164]

O God, grant that we may desire to do your will, deny-

ing our fleshly will and putting it to death.[165] And when
our last hour comes, grant that the eternal name of Jesus
may be our last word and sigh. May we fall asleep in him,
blessed, and rise at the last day unto eternal life, through
Jesus Christ. Amen. [142]

☩

A Morning Prayer

O Lord, merciful, gracious God, Father of eternal light
and comfort, whose goodness and faithfulness is new each
morning![166] To you we declare our praise, honor, and gratitude for the treasured light of day, for protecting us graciously during the night, and for granting us a gentle sleep
and rest.

May we now once again arise in your grace and love,
under your care and protection, and make use of the cher-
ished light of day in a useful and joyous manner.

Above all, enlighten us with the eternal light, our
Lord Jesus Christ, that he might shine in us with his grace
and knowledge. Preserve in our hearts the light of faith.
Grant increase to this faith and strengthen it. Awaken
your love in us, and confirm the hope. Grant us true humility that we may walk in the footsteps of our Lord Jesus
Christ. In our every act allow your godly fear in us to be
seen by others.

Dispel all spiritual darkness in us and blindness of
heart. Today and every day, safeguard us against supersti-
tion and idolatry, against arrogance and blasphemy of
your name, against despising your Word, against disobe-
dience and loathsome anger, so that the sun might not

[143] set upon our anger this day.[167]

Protect us from enmity, hate, and envy, from disorder and unrighteousness, from falsehood, lies, and damaging greed, and from every evil desire. Awaken in us a hunger and thirst for you and your righteousness. Teach us to act according to your pleasure, for you are our God.

May your good Spirit lead us onto a smooth path. We commit ourselves to you. Bless all our actions that they may bring honor to your name and be useful to our neighbor. Make us instruments of your grace. Permit us to continue safely in our calling, and restrain all those who would obstruct our walk of life.

Safeguard us against slander and the liar's murderous arrows. Accompany us at all times with your grace. Hold your hand above us constantly, whether we are walking or standing, awake or asleep. Safeguard us also against evil, painful sickness, and deadly epidemics. Bless all our nourishment, provide for us in all our human needs in accord with your will, and keep us from misusing your gifts.

Protect us from war, hunger, pestilence, and from an evil and premature death. Guard our souls, indeed, our going out and our coming in forevermore.[168] Bestow upon us a [144] blessed end. May we with longing and joy await the good day of the last judgment and the glorious appearing of our Lord Jesus Christ.[169]

May God the Father bless and keep us in Jesus Christ, and in his holy and good Spirit. Amen.

✠

A Prayer of Devout Parents for Their Children

O Lord! dear faithful God and Father, Creator and Sustainer of all creatures! Grant your grace also to us that we may raise our children in the discipline and admonition of the Lord and in all righteousness, and that we may lead the way in all fear of God and in virtue.

May you also grant grace to our children and impart the gift of the Holy Spirit to them. Thus may they in turn accept our instruction in the love and fear of God, making it their own. Kindle in them the true fear of God, which is the beginning of wisdom, so that thereafter they may live by that wisdom and so remain forever in line with your promise.[170]

Bless them with your true knowledge, and safeguard them from every idolatry and false teaching. May they grow up in the true saving faith [145] and genuine divine salvation, and remain therein until the end. Give them a believing, obedient heart, also true wisdom and understanding, that they may grow and increase in years and in favor with God and their fellow human beings.[171]

Oh! plant in their hearts the love of your divine Word, so that they may be thoughtful in prayer and worship services, showing respect to ministers of the Word and to everyone. May they be upright in their actions and conduct, disciplined, righteous, and faithful in living out God's salvation. Indeed, may they reflect love and gentleness toward all people.

Safeguard them against every form of torment of the evil world, so that they may not be led astray by bad company. May they not fall into wickedness or offend others.

Be their protection in every danger so they do not suddenly perish.

Preserve and grant increase to our congregation here on earth, through us, our children, and our descendants. Thus may we with them praise you in your eternal heavenly kingdom, as part of that multitude that no one could number, who carried palm branches in their hands. Indeed, may we sing the new song with joy, to the praise of your holy name.[172] In the holy name of Jesus. Amen. [252][173]

✠

Fine Prayers, Rich in Spirit, from the Canadian *Christenpflicht*

Morning Prayer

Merciful, good God and Father! once again you have allowed the rising sun to shine[174] upon good and evil! May praise and thanksgiving be declared to you, O good God! for your fatherly grace and for the protection and blessing which I have enjoyed this past night. Let me enjoy your blessing this day as well.

Illuminate my dark heart with your light of grace, so I may examine my faults and mistakes and learn to recognize them sufficiently. Shelter me today under the protection of your grace. Fill my heart with your divine love, with true humility and modesty. Strengthen me in faith, and let me grow and improve in all goodness from day to day.

Place my frailty and mortality squarely before my eyes, so I may constantly be on guard. Set your Holy Spirit to watch over my heart, senses, and thoughts, that if this should be my last day in this woeful world, I may be alert and [253] attain peace of soul.

Thus into your hands I commit myself, body and soul and all that I have. It is no longer mine; it is totally yours. In times of distress and need, grant me patience. During times of testing and temptation, grant me strength and vigor. During prosperous days filled with well-being, grant me a thankful heart. And protect me from all evil, here on earth and there in eternity, through Jesus Christ. Amen.

☩
Evening Prayer

Merciful, gracious God and Father, I declare to you my praise and thanksgiving for creating day and night and separating light from darkness. You have made the day for work and the night for rest, so humanity along with the animals can be refreshed.

I praise and extol you for all your works and good deeds which you have bestowed upon me through your divine grace and protection during this past day. You have also allowed me to overcome and surmount the burdens and troubles of the day.

It is enough, dear Father, that each day has its own burdens. You are always helping to lift from us one burden after the other, until we finally come to rest on that eternal day when all troubles and burdens cease.

I thank you from my heart for all the good I have received from your hand today. O Lord! I am too limited to absorb all your mercy which you bestow upon me daily. I thank you also for turning aside the evil which I might have encountered this day. [254] I thank you for covering and preserving me under the protection of the Most High, under the shadow of the Almighty, from all misfortune and from grievous sins.

From the heart I pray, as a child, forgive me all the sins which I have committed today, in thought, word, and deed. Much evil have I done; much opportunity for good have I let slip by.

Oh, be gracious to me, my God, be gracious to me. Let all my sins die to me this day. Grant that I may rise up again, ever more God-fearing, more holy, more devout, and more righteous. May my slumber not be a sinful sleep but a holy sleep, so that my soul and my inner spirit might awaken to you, speak to you, and relate to you.

Bless my sleep, as that of the patriarch Jacob when in a dream he saw the ladder of heaven and the holy angels, and received the blessing.[175] May I speak of you when I lie down in bed, and reflect on you when I awaken.[176] May your name and memory always remain in my heart, whether I am asleep or awake.

Grant that I may not be frightened by the dread of the night, nor fearful of sudden terror or the storm winds of the ungodly. Instead, may I sleep peacefully. Protect me from nightmares, from the enemy breaking in, from fire and flood.

Behold, the One who keeps us does not slumber; behold, the Guardian of Israel neither slumbers nor sleeps. O God! be my Shadow over my right hand, that the sun may not scorch me by day, nor the moon by night.[177] May your holy watchers protect me, and your angels surround and assist me.[178] [255]

May your holy angel awaken me again at the right time, like the prophet Elijah when he slept under the juniper tree,[179] and like Peter when he slept in prison between the guards.[180] May the holy angels appear in my sleep as they did to Joseph and to the wise men from the East,[181] so I may know that I too am in the company of the holy angels. And when my hour of death is at hand, bestow upon me a blessed sleep and a blessed rest in Jesus Christ, my Lord. Amen.

☦

Evening Prayer

Praise and thanksgiving be to you, O almighty God and Father! for your protection and blessing, and for all the good which I have enjoyed during this past day! I would gladly enter the inner sanctum of my heart to worship you in spirit and in truth. But it is still so full of impurity, for today I have been burdened with many scattered thoughts. Also, in my actions and life, I have not responded in the best way, for I am full of defects and mistakes; I am poor and miserable.

Although I am only dust and ashes, I still have dared to call upon your holy name. I pray and woefully implore you, O my God! forgive me all my transgressions and mistakes with which I have offended you. Cleanse [256] my heart of all fleshly and worldly desires! Fill me with your Holy Spirit! Illuminate me with your light of grace! Thus may I come to know how my hidden mistakes look in the light.

Truly soften my heart, making it the bearer of remorse

and sorrow. Through your grace bring about true regret and repentance in my soul. Give me the true, living, and saving faith. Kindle the fire of your divine love in my soul, and let it glow and burn until my selfishness is completely consumed.

I also pray for all people, for all the poor and unknown sinners, for all my enemies and opponents, for all the sick, for all the widows and the forsaken. You know the needs of each one, and may you aid each one who needs your help.

Now I lay my body down into the arms of your grace and mercy and commit myself, body and soul, into your hands. Protect me with your holy angels. Bless and shield me from all evil, whether I am asleep or awake. Teach me to reflect upon my nothingness, my dying, and my death. Finally receive my immortal soul into eternal joy and rest! This I pray, O almighty God and Father, in the name of Jesus Christ. Amen.

✠

Prayer of a Remorseful Sinner

O Lord! almighty, all-powerful God! In my distress I turn to you and call to you in the [257] name of Jesus Christ. Have mercy upon me, poor creature, for I find myself laden with sins and impurity. My senses are scattered and my thoughts are too earthly and worldly. I am also finding little strength truly to repent, for my desires and inclinations for evil are strong, and my inclination and love for the good is very weak.

Therefore, I come to you as a laden sinner, placing myself before the throne of your grace, on your footstool, with bowed heart. I hope you will hear my prayer and take me, poor as I am, under the protection of your grace. For I acknowledge that I am dust and ashes! I have no strength to do good and forsake evil.

All good gifts come from you. Therefore, take from me my worldly heart, inclined to do evil, and give me a new and grateful heart, with a disposition which truly accepts remorse and sorrow. Fill me with your Holy Spirit. Anoint me through and through with your divine love, O eternal Wisdom!

Make your Word truly living and mighty in my soul through the true faith. Free me from all bonds and cords with which I still find myself shackled from time to time. Lead and direct me on the right path to eternal bliss. Guard and protect me from all evil, here in time and even to eternity. Amen. [258]

☨

Prayer for a Blessed End

Most beloved Father in heaven! oh, what evil have I brought forth in my short life! Few are the days of my life, and many are my sins. The least of my time I have lived unto you; the most and the best of my time I have wasted in vanity. Oh, how much good have I let slip by, and in comparison how much evil have I gathered, thereby staining my body and my soul!

Oh, most beloved Father, forgive everything out of grace! Oh, gentle Redeemer, cover up all this with the robe of your innocence and righteousness! Oh, heal my wounded soul with your comfort! Teach me to bear in mind that my time here must end, that my life has a goal, and that I will need to depart.[182]

Behold, my days are the width of a hand, and my life is as nothing before you. Oh, how absolutely empty are all people who still live so self-assuredly! They go about like a shadow. They are concerned with heaping up earthly wealth, and do not know into whose hands it will come.

Now, Lord, in whom shall I place my trust? My hope rests in you. Save me from all my sins, and let me not become the laughingstock of fools. I want to remain quiet and not open my mouth. You will certainly save me, for I am both your pilgrim and your citizen, as were all my ancestors.

Indeed, I am a stranger. Here I have no lasting place, but look for the place that is to come.[183] I am like a day-laborer who longs for shade.[184] I know you have [259] counted all my days, and have written into your book those days still to come, which have not yet come to be.[185] Oh, let me realize that my life is a pilgrimage, a passage-way through this vale of tears.

May I not be detained on this way. Oh, my dear Father! when my time is fulfilled which you have set for me, when my days have reached their goal that you have written into your book, then grant me a blessed and joyful passage from this life. Cast out of me the love for this world and the desire to live longer. Give me a joyful heart, ready to depart. Dispel every fear and dismay. Protect me from the temptation of the enemy. Arm my soul with the weapons of your righteousness, with the shield of faith and the helmet of salvation.[186]

For you, O Lord Jesus Christ, are my wisdom, righteousness, salvation, and redemption; my life, comfort, peace, and joy. May I depart in faith, love, and hope.[187] Kindle in me a holy thirst for eternal life, that just as the deer cries for fresh water, so also my soul cries to you and thirsts for you, the living God. I speak from the heart: When will I come to you, that I may see your face?[188]

Let me reflect on how lovely your dwellings are.[189] Let my body and my soul rejoice in you, the living God. Let my poor soul, like a scared little bird, find a home where it may remain eternally, at your altar, which is the bitter suffering and death and merit of my Redeemer, Jesus Christ.

Lord of Hosts, my King [260] and my God, refresh my memory of the innocent death of Christ, my Savior. Oh, my Redeemer, Christ Jesus! in my weakness and in the throes of death, show me your suffering, your wounds, your welts, your crown of thorns, your cross and death. Show me your torn side, your pierced hands and feet, which are streams of pure joy and comfort.[190]

Let me hear in my heart the comforting words which you spoke on the cross: Today you shall be with me in paradise.[191] Oh, my sole Physician, heal me, for I am the wounded one who has fallen among the thieves. Bind up my wounds.[192] Heal me of all my hurts through the agony of your death and your bloody sweat. Soften my mortal terror through your death. Bless my death.

You are the resurrection and the life; even though they die, those who believe in you will live.[193] The souls of the righteous are in your hand, and no torment of death can touch them.[194] From now on, blessed are the dead who die in the Lord. They are resting from their work.[195] O Lord! let my soul find true rest in you. Call me to yourself.

Reach out your hand to me as you did to Peter on the water, that I might not sink.[196] Say, Come to me. I want to revive you.

Call out to me, Lord, for I have entered evening time.[197] Lay me down in my little bedroom. Call me to yourself, from darkness into light, from misery into the true fatherland, from serving sin into eternal freedom and righteousness, from death to life, from the stormy sea of this world onto the [261] shore of the true fatherland. Lead me through the fearful sea of physical death into the true Promised Land.

Oh, save me from this sinful, impure life! I long for the pure, holy, divine life, where there is no sin, where only pure righteousness abounds. Lead me from this restless life into the true, eternal, blessed rest, where there is no toil or work, no sickness or death, no cares or sadness. There God is all in all. There God is our food, our clothing, our home and holy dwelling, our delight, our joy, our life.

There I shall experience a glorious exchange, when I shall inherit eternal, abiding glory in place of my earthly trouble, misery, and woe; eternal joy for this temporal sadness, immortality for this mortality, heavenly strength for this frailty, eternal health for this sickness, eternal life for this temporal life. Thus Christ is my life, and death is my gain.[198]

Oh! how great is my desire to lay aside my mortal body and to put on an immortal body, my desire to take off the corruptible and put on the incorruptible, my desire to plant my weak body into the earth as a kernel of wheat so I may rise again in power. I will gladly pass through the disgrace of death and be placed in the grave, so that I may arise in glory.

Oh, now be content, my soul! for the Lord is doing a good thing for you. He has rescued you from death, your eyes from tears, your feet from slipping. Now I will [262] walk in the land of the blessed forever and ever.

Oh, open to me soon the door of life, Lord Jesus Christ! You are the door, and whoever enters through you will be saved.[199] I am to come to you, my heavenly Bridegroom, for the wedding. You are standing at the door, waiting for me. In preparation, therefore, I put on my wedding garment of the righteousness of Jesus Christ, and the flaming white garment of the eternal Sabbath, so that my soul may appear before you pure, unspotted, and without fault.[200]

So let me hear your word of joy: Come here, you who are blessed of the Lord, inherit the kingdom of your Father, prepared for you from the beginning, and enter into the joy of your Lord. Amen.[201]

☩

Prayer for a Funeral Service
Before the Sermon

Almighty, Eternal God! Lord over life and death! You are God from eternity. Your years endure and have no end. You alone are immortal. We, however, are transient and mortal. You remain who you are. We, however, are perishable. We come into being and pass away, flourish and wither, as your almighty will commands us. From you, our God and Creator of all things! we have breath, life, and being; from you, we have our destiny, measured days, and life span, which [263] we cannot overstep.[202]

Father and God of your redeemed children! teach us all to consider well that we are transient, that we are mortal. Here we have no abiding place, but must look for the place that is to come, that we may become wise.[203]

We have just come from the grave of our friend whom we have laid to rest.[204] Our purpose is to find comfort in the Word of the Lord concerning ___ [his/her] passing, and to remind ourselves of our own mortality. We want to secure our calling and election with you, and to give ourselves completely to the working out of salvation, without which no one will see you. Thus may we enter the promised rest of eternal life.[205]

O my God! in this hallowed hour, infuse into our hearts the whole weight of death and eternity, for your glory, and for amending our own lives. May we see and know the futility of all earthly and fleeting things, to which we often attach our hearts so firmly. So may we be awakened from the sleep of self-assuredness and sin.

Impart power and strength to your Word and your teachings about our mortality, for all souls still hanging onto this earth, forgetting life's end, death and the grave, and ignoring the fear of God. Almighty One, if they continue to despise your saving grace, speak to them in their hearts with the powerful word of eternity, and show them their evil actions. Remind them that they need to turn to God before the night of death comes, when no one can do good or carry it out.[206]

May this view of death be a comforting, heartfelt teaching for all who stand in the state of grace, and who in faith [264] are hoping for the redemption of their body. May it be a foretaste of the coming majesty of God, which shall be revealed to them through Jesus Christ. Amen. Our Father . . . [the Lord's Prayer].

⛭

Prayer After the Funeral Sermon

Almighty, great God! Creator of all things, Lord and Master over all that your wise hand has created and prepared! We mortals! being dust and ashes, have been reminded of our nothingness through the departure of our friend and through your holy Word. This draws our attention to our duties, how we should prepare ourselves for our end, so that death may not find us in an unredeemed[207] condition when God, according to his counsel, calls us also to our eternal destiny.

The time of our pilgrimage is short! Few and evil are our days here on earth. Our years lead toward death as if flying away from this life. Before we notice it, the time of life is spent, and we hurry after our friend to the grave, humanity's common bed of rest.

O God! our most gracious Father, stamp this deeply into our souls. Thus may we truly watch and care for our eternal salvation. May we be prepared when the Lord of the house comes and summons us to give an account for the talents of grace and gifts entrusted to us. Help us not to fall asleep in foolish self-assurance and then miss meeting the Bridegroom. Instead, may we constantly provide the lamps of our [265] hearts with the spirit and the oil of faith, committing ourselves every hour to God and to his holy will. Thus may God usher us as his very own into the eternal feast of joy.[208]

Just like our friend, after our final breath, one after the other of us goes from the land of mortality into eternity. Every dead body we see reminds us of death and calls out to us: Today, me; tomorrow, you. Therefore, help us, dearest God! that we who are ripe for death might well consider daily the one thing we need:[209] to secure our condition of grace with Jesus, and to seek forgiveness of sin through his divine merit. Thus may we attain reconciliation and peace with God, so we do not miss the promise of entering into his rest.[210]

When the hour of death comes for us, Lord Jesus! help us in the last battle to conquer in faith, and to die blessed. Lead us into the delight of your eternal majesty, where in undisturbed peace we may serve you eternally in pure immortality, like the angels, lifting up your high praise. Amen. (Matthew 6:9-13.)[211]

Our Father who art in heaven,
Hallowed be thy name.
Thy kingdom come.
Thy will be done on earth,
    as it is in heaven.
Give us this day our daily bread.
And forgive us our debts,
    as we forgive our debtors.
And lead us not into temptation,
    but deliver us from evil.
For thine is the kingdom and the power
    and the glory, forever. Amen.

⚜

Editions of *Christenpflicht*

This list of known editions of *Die ernsthafte Christenpflicht* was compiled through years of research by David Luthy and used here with his permission.

Abbreviations

F.	*France*
G.	*Germany*
n.p.	*no printing place given*
n.d.	*no printing date given*
repr.	*reprint*
S.	*Switzerland*
U.C.	*Upper Canada*

• • •

European German Editions

1708	n.p.	[1798]	Saarburg [G.]
1716	n.p.	1816	Zweibrücken, G.
1718	n.p.	1832	Basel, S.
1727	n.p.	1833	n.p.
1730	n.p.	1837	Zweibrücken, G.
1739	Kaiserslautern, G.	n.d.	Zweibrücken, G.
1740	n.p.	1840	Reinach bei Basel, S.
1753	n.p.	1852	Regensburg, G.
1768	n.p.	1869	Neuwyl bei
1781	n.p.		Saint-Louis, F.
1781	Pirmasens, G.	1869	Zweibrücken, G.
1787	Herborn, G.		
1796	n.p.		

Canadian German Editions

1846	Berlin, U.C.	[1979]	photo reprint of 1952 ed.
1878	Berlin, Ont.	1992	Aylmer, Ont.
1908	Berlin, Ont.	1994	Aylmer, Ont.
1952	Kitchener, Ont.		

• • •

USA German Editions

1745	Ephrata, Pa.	1953	Lancaster, Pa.
1770	Ephrata, Pa.	1955	Scottdale, Pa.
1785	Ephrata, Pa.	1958	Scottdale, Pa.
1808	Ephrata, Pa.	1961	Lancaster, Pa.
1810	Somerset, Pa.	1961	Scottdale, Pa.
1826	Lancaster, Pa.	1964	Lancaster, Pa.
1826	Wooster, Ohio	1965	Scottdale, Pa.
1828	Canton, Ohio	1967	Scottdale, Pa.
1839	Canton, Ohio	1968	Lancaster, Pa.
1841	Lancaster, Pa.	1971	Scottdale, Pa.
1852	Lancaster, Pa.	1972	Lancaster, Pa.
1862	Lancaster, Pa.	1974	Scottdale, Pa.
1868	Lancaster, Pa.	1975	Scottdale, Pa.
1875	Lancaster, Pa.	1976	Lancaster, Pa.
1886	Elkhart, Ind.	1978	Scottdale, Pa.
1892	Lancaster, Pa.	1980	Scottdale, Pa.
1894	Elkhart Ind.	1982	Scottdale, Pa.
1904	Lancaster Pa.	1984	Scottdale, Pa.
1907	Elkhart, Ind.	1986	Scottdale, Pa.
1914	Elkhart, Ind.	1987	Scottdale, Pa.
1915	Scottdale, Pa.	1987	Lancaster, Pa.
1921	Arthur, Ill.	1987	Gordonville, Pa.
1924	Scottdale, Pa.	1989	Scottdale, Pa.
1927	Lancaster, Pa.	1989	Bloomfield, Iowa
1937	Scottdale, Pa.	1990	Scottdale, Pa.
1939	Lancaster, Pa.	1991	Scottdale, Pa.
1945	Scottdale, Pa.	1992	Lancaster, Pa.
1945	Lancaster, Pa.	1994	Fredericksburg, Ohio
1953	Lancaster, Pa.		

Selections in English

A Devoted Christian's Prayer Book		1984	Aylmer, Ont.
[1964]	Daviess Co., Ind.	1990	Aylmer, Ont.
1967	Aylmer, Ont.	1995	Aylmer, Ont.
1976	Aylmer, Ont.		

• • •

English Editions
Prayer Book for Earnest Christians
1997   Scottdale, Pa.

✠

Notes

1. Original title: *Die ernsthafte Christenpflicht* (The duty [obligation] of earnest Christians), available in German, bound with prayers in the first part and in an appendix, all translated here (Aylmer, Ont.; and LaGrange, Ind.: Pathway Publishers, 1992 or latest printing). Several other sections bound in the 1992 German volume are not translated here: "A Short Explanation of the Faith of Defenseless Christians," by Tieleman Tielen van Sittert, from 1664; the 1632 Dordrecht Confession of Faith; "Rules of a Godly Life," from the *Geistliches Lustgärtlein* prayer book of 1787 or earlier; and four hymns. From 1927, Lancaster Amish usually omit "Rules" from their editions because they include "Rules" in *Lustgärtlein*. See note 3, below.

2. Information in a letter of Oct. 16, 1995, from David Luthy, Editor, Pathway Publishers, R.R. 4, Aylmer, Ontario N5H 2R3, Canada. See "Editions of *Christenpflicht*" on pages 133-135, above; and notes 173 and 204, below.

3. For further information, see the following: David Luthy, "A History of *Die ernsthafte Christenpflicht*," *Family Life*, Feb. 1981, 19-23. Robert Friedmann, *"Ernsthafte Christenpflicht,"* in *The Mennonite Encyclopedia* (ME), 2 (Scottdale, Pa.: Mennonite Publishing House/Herald Press, 1956): 244-245, analyzing the prayers and how this volume fits into the larger Anabaptist-Mennonite publishing history. Robert Friedmann, *Mennonite Piety Through the Centuries*, Studies in Anabaptist and Mennonite History, 7 (Goshen, Ind.: Mennonite Historical Society: Herald Press, 1949), chapter on "Mennonite Prayer Books," 176-202, especially 189-195. Harold S. Bender, "Prayer Books, Mennonite," in *ME*, 4 (1959): 211-212. For a list of known editions or printings, see pages 133-135, below.

4. This first prayer is a revision of the tenth prayer found in the Swiss Mennonite devotional book *Güldene Aepffel in silbern Schalen*

(Golden apples in silver bowls), 1702 (see Prov. 25:11). There it is entitled "Form for a Morning Prayer, to Be Offered Reverently Before God, with Bowed Knees of the Heart" (see note 12, below). *Golden Apples* included prayers collected by Leenaert Clock in the first distinct Mennonite prayer book, in Dutch, *Forma eenigher Christenlijker ghebeden* (A formulary of several Christian prayers), 1625; it was published in German as *Formulier etlicher Gebäthe*, 1660. See "Prayer Books," *ME*, 4:211-212; and Friedmann, *Mennonite Piety*, 156-165, 182-189. For basis in Scripture, see Gen. 1—3; Ps. 90.

5. Compare Rev. 1:14.

6. Here some older editions had "etc.," meaning that the one praying should complete the list, according to the given needs of the moment.

7. Revised from prayer 13 of *Golden Apples*, entitled "A Form for Evening Prayer, to be Spoken with a Reverent Heart and Bowed Knees," originally from Clock.

8. *Word* is regularly capitalized in these prayers because it usually seems to refer to the Bible. But certainly it often includes God being heard contemporaneously, as in preaching. For "know not what they are doing," see Luke 23:34.

9. This clause, "die uns Dein heiliges Wort nach Deinem Willen mögen verkündigen (that they may proclaim to us your holy Word according to your will)," is an addition, not found in the original Clock prayer. This suggests a shift in the vision for mission from "those on the outside" to "us."

10. Original: "until we die blessed." See Rev. 14:13, assuring that those who die in the Lord are "selig (blessed, saved)."

11. Revised from prayer 2 of *Golden Apples*, entitled "Form for a General Prayer After the Sermon." See note 4.

12. This clause, "die Kniee unseres Herzens beugen (bending the knees of our heart)," expresses depth of feeling and is modeled on The Prayer of Manasseh 11 (in the Apocrypha). One could paraphrase it: "humbling our heart." Compare Dan. 5:22; Joel 2:13.

13. Matt. 6:9-13, adapted from the KJV.

14. See Rom. 5:6-11; Eph. 2:1-10; etc.

15. See Col. 3:14.

16. Original has "Männer (men)."

17. See Eph. 4:11-16; 2 Tim. 3:17.

18. On the "book of life," see Ps. 69:28; Dan. 12:1; Phil. 4:3; Rev. 3:5; 13:8; 17:8; 20:12, 15; 21:27.

19. Repeatedly these prayers mention the "truehearted" and "goodhearted." These terms refer specifically to friendly non-Anabaptist neighbors and relatives who helped the Swiss Anabaptists and sheltered them during persecution. They sympathized with the Anabaptists but had not committed themselves to believers baptism nor submitted to the discipline of the congregation. See *Letters of the Amish Division: A Sourcebook*, trans. and ed. John D. Roth, with Joe Springer (Goshen, Ind.: Mennonite Historical Society, 1993), 11.

20. See Heb. 12:1; Col. 3:8; 1 Tim. 6:10; etc.

21. See note 16.

22. On keeping faith forever, see Ps. 146:6, Luther's *Bibel* and NRSV; compare "keeping covenant" in 1 Kings 8:23; 2 Chron. 6:14; Neh. 6:32; Dan. 9:4.

23. See Gal. 5:19-21; and also 1 Cor. 5:10-11; 6:9-10; 2 Cor. 12:20-21; Eph. 4:31; 5:3-5; Col. 3:5-8; 1 Tim. 6:3-10; 2 Tim. 3:2-4; Phil. 3:19; Exod. 20:4-6.

24. Compare Gen. 6:5. Under some influence of Pietism (from 1670), "lowly worm that I am" shows humility. Note Isaac Watts (1707), "Alas! and did my Savior bleed? / And did my Sov'reign die? / Would He devote that sacred head / For such a worm as I?" See also Ps. 22:6; Job 17:14; 25:6; Isa. 40:22; 41:14; 66:24; Mark 9:48.

25. See 1 Cor. 10:13.

26. See note 16.

27. See Isa. 6:7.

28. Compare Acts 4:24-30; Ps. 2:1-2.

29. See note 22, above, and Ps. 24:1.

30. See Rev. 5:6-10; Isa. 53:7; John 1:29, 36; 1 Pet. 1:19.

31. See Matt. 5:8; Ps. 24:4; Heb. 12:14.

32. Reference to being "reborn" or the "new birth from above" occurs repeatedly in these prayers. See John 3:3-9; 1:13; 1 Pet. 1:23; 1 John 2:29; 3:9; 4:7; 5:1, 4, 18.

33. This prayer relates to 1 Cor. 6:12-20.

34. See 1 Cor. 10:13.

35. Eph. 4:3.

36. See note 16. For "Lord of the harvest," see Matt 9:37-38; Luke 10:2.

37. See Col. 3:14.

38. See note 23, above.

39. See note 22, above, and Ps. 24:1.

40. See Eph. 6:10-17; Ps. 90:5-6; 139:23-24; Heb. 4:12-13; etc.

41. See Lev. 19:18; Matt. 7:12; 19:19; 22:39-40; Mark 12:31; Luke 6:31; 10:27; Rom. 13:8-10; James 2:11.

42. Matt. 6:33.

43. See 2 Tim. 4:6-8.

44. In the Apocrypha, see the books of Susanna, Judith, and 2 Maccabees 6—7. In the Old Testament, see Dan. 6; Jonah 1—2; Dan. 3.

45. See 1 Cor. 10:13.

46. For the wedding banquet and the wise virgins, see Matt. 25:1-13.

47. See Matt. 5:9-12, 43-48; 25:34-40; Rom. 12:9-21.

48. See note 16.

49. See note 16.

50. This startling statement reflects the Anabaptists' position that young children are part of the kingdom of God (Matt. 19:13-15; Mark 10:13-16; Luke 18:15-17). When mature, they must be called to make an adult decision and a public commitment to Christ in believers baptism. The desire is that they will receive God's mercy and live as disciples of Christ. If God takes them (see Job 1:21) as young children, they are spiritually safe. But if they grow up and reject God's mercy, they are spiritually lost. Spiritual life with God is worth more than physical life; see Matt. 5:29-30; 16:24-27; Rom. 8:36-39; etc.

51. On shining as a light and bringing glory to God, see Matt. 5:14-16.

52. See 2 Cor. 6:14—7:1, against such ties or partnerships.

53. See Ps. 90:1-2.

54. See Matt. 10:16, 22.

55. Matt. 10:23.

56. Gen. 28:10-17; the angels of God met Jacob as he fled toward Haran.

57. John 15:18-20.

58. See 2 Tim. 3:12.

59. Selections from 1 Cor. 4:9-13.

60. Matt. 5:10-12.

61. See 2 Cor. 4:9; Acts 14:22.

62. See 1 Pet. 4:13-14; Isa. 52:5; James 2:7; etc.

63. The "apple of the eye" is the precious pupil of the eye. See Ps. 17:8; 57:1; Zech. 2:8.

64. Ps. 24:1.

65. Ps. 146:5-10.

66. On a plumb line of righteousness, see 2 Kings 21:13-15; Amos 7:7-9; Isa. 28:17.

67. See Rom. 7—8, especially 8:13.

68. For this paragraph and the next, see Gal. 2:20; 1 Cor. 6:19.

69. See Col. 1:15.

70. See Rom. 6:4-14; 8:5-25; Gal. 2:19-20.

71. Adapted from Col. 1:12-14.

72. See Rev. 20:1-3, "bottomless pit"; Heb. 13:20, "eternal covenant."

73. See 1 Cor. 1:30.

74. Rom. 14:17; 1 Cor. 6:19-20.

75. See Ps. 8:1-2; Matt. 21:16.

76. This passage is based on Ps. 45:1-8.

77. Ps. 24:7.

78. This passage is based on Ps. 110:1-4. Compare Gen. 14:18.

79. For this passage, see Matt. 25:31-34; John 17:24.

80. See 1 Sam. 2:6-8; Luke 1:52.

81. See, for example, 2 Thess. 3:6-13.

82. This passage relates to Matt. 6:25-33.

83. See, for examples, Deut. 14:29; 24:19-21; James 1:27.

84. See Ps. 113:7-8.

85. Prov. 28:6.

86. Tobit 4:21, in the Apocrypha.

87. Ps. 37:25.

88. See 1 Tim. 6:7.

89. Referring to the Preacher in Eccles. 5:10—6:9. Compare 1 Cor. 7:17; Ps. 113:7.

90. Matt. 8:20.

91. Ps. 27:13-14.

92. See Rev. 8:1; 6:15-17; 16:19-20; 20:11.

93. Compare Gal. 6:16, "Israel of God," and 1 Cor. 10:18 (NRSV footnote), "Israel according to the flesh."

94. Adapted from Eph. 1:3-22; compare 3:14-21.

95. See Isa. 11:2; Eph. 1:3.

96. See 1 Pet. 1:18-19.

97. Selected from The Prayer of Manasseh 9-14, in the Apocrypha, which is intended to supply the prayer mentioned in 2 Chron. 33:10-13, 18.

98. Or, "I humble my heart." See note 12, above.

99. Daniel desires the restoration of Jerusalem; Dan. 9:16, 19. Compare Paul's remarks on the Jerusalem from above, in Gal. 4:24-26. The prayer can be adapted to current needs.

100. Matt. 9:18; Mark 5:23; Luke 8:41-42.

101. Matt. 8:8-9; Luke 7:6-8.

102. Ps. 25:17, in Luther's *Bibel.*

103. Compare Ps. 116:3.

104. On Mary Magdalene, see Luke 8:2. The prayer follows an uncertain tradition of identifying her with the sinner woman of Luke 7:36-50. On the hem of the garment, see Matt. 9:20; 14:36.

105. See 2 Cor. 12:9.

106. Based on Ps. 102:5 in Luther's *Bibel* = 102:4 in English Bibles.

107. See Jonah 2; Mark 10:46-52; Luke 18:35-43.

108. In theological and biblical usage, "Anfechtung" usually means "temptation," which fits the misery over sin in this prayer. One might translate, "attack of anxiety," yet it comes chiefly out of awareness of sin. For *Anfechtung,* see Luther's *Bibel:* Matt. 26:41; Acts 20:19; James 1:2, 12; etc.

109. Ps. 51:10.

110. Revised from prayer 1 of *Golden Apples.* See note 4.

111. Deut. 8:3; Matt. 4:4; Luke 4:4.

112. Revised from prayer 3 of *Golden Apples.*

113. Original: "clothed with this dwelling." See 2 Cor. 5:1-10.

114. See John 14:13-14.

115. Col. 2:3.

116. See Ps. 80:3, 7, 19.

117. Revised from prayer 4 of *Golden Apples.*

118. See Eph. 4:13, 15.

119. See Phil. 1:11; 2 Tim. 3:17; Heb. 4:12-13.

120. Revised from prayer 5 of *Golden Apples.*

121. See Gen. 3; Rom. 5; Gal. 4:4-5.

122. Rom. 8:32; John 3:16.

123. See note 12, above.

124. These prayers repeatedly call for the renunciation of the world, the flesh, and the devil, traditionally included in promises made by those being baptized on confession of faith. See Luke 14:26-27; James 4:7; 1 John 2:15-16; 3:8-10.

125. Eph. 5:25-32; Rev. 19:7-8; 21:2, 9. For "kings," see Rev. 1:6.

126. Rom. 8:17.

127. Rom. 8:13; Col. 3:5-10.

128. Revised from prayer 6 of *Golden Apples*.

129. Revised from prayer 7 of *Golden Apples*.

130. Revised from prayer 8 of *Golden Apples*. See Heb. 13:20.

131. Revised from prayer 9 of *Golden Apples*. See Gen. 2:1-25.

132. Matt. 19:3-9; 1 Cor. 7:2.

133. Revised from prayer 12 of *Golden Apples*.

134. Revised from prayer 15 of *Golden Apples*.

135. Revised from prayer 16 of *Golden Apples*. See Ps. 145:15-16.

136. Revised from prayer 17 of *Golden Apples*.

137. Revised from prayer 18 of *Golden Apples*, written about 1625. On sickness as the Lord's discipline, see Pss. 6; 38; etc. Compare Prov. 3:11-12; Heb. 12:5-11.

138. For the blanks, supply the name of the sick person or a suitable pronoun, he/she, him/his/her. In the rest of this prayer, Clock, the author, focuses on the individual sick person. All of Clock's prayers were intended only to provide suggestions. Since this prayer covers a range of possible situations, the one praying can choose what seems appropriate and omit the rest.

139. Literally: "stands before the eyes."

140. See Isa. 53; 2 Cor. 5:21.

141. See 1 Pet. 1:18-19; Rev. 1:5; 7:14.

142. See Jer. 23:5-6; 33:15-16; Rom. 3:21-26; 1 Cor. 1:30; 2 Cor. 5:21; Phil. 3:9; etc.

143. Luke 23:39-43.

144. Original: "Gnadenstuhl (mercy seat)," as in Luther's *Bibel:* Heb. 4:16; 9:5; Rom. 3:25; Exod. 26:34; Lev. 16:12-15.

145. See note 12, above.

146. Literally: "my misdeed is the evil illness."

147. See Isa. 53.

148. See 1 Pet. 1:19; 2 Kings 19:35; 1 Chron. 21:12-30; Exod. 12:5, 13.

149. At the blanks, supply the name or pronoun for the deceased person.

150. Heb. 9:27.

151. Ps. 90:12.

152. Based on 2 Tim. 4:7-8.

153. See Luke 23:46.

154. See James 1:17; Phil. 2:13.

155. Heb. 12:2.

156. See 1 Cor. 12:11.

157. See Phil. 1:6, 9-11.

158. See 2 Cor. 4:7.

159. Based on Rom. 12:1-2.

160. Based on Eph. 3:16-19.

161. Based on Ps. 43:3; 2 Tim. 4:7; 1 Tim. 6:12-13; 1:5; Ps. 25:5.

162. See 1 John 2:16.

163. Based on Rom. 14:17.

164. Phil. 4:7.

165. See Col. 3:5.

166. See Lam. 3:23.

167. See Eph. 4:26.

168. Based on Ps. 121:8.

169. See Titus 4:13; 2 Tim. 4:8.

170. See Eph. 6:4; Prov. 1:7.

171. Based on Luke 2:52 in Luther's *Bibel*; see NRSV and KJV. The Greek text means "increase in height . . ." or "increase in age."

172. See Rev. 5:9-10; 7:9-12; 14:3.

173. The following prayers are translated from the "Anhang (Appendix). Schöne geistreiche Gebete aus der kanadischen *Christenpflicht*," as found in *Die ernsthafte Christenpflicht* (Aylmer, Ontario; LaGrange, Indiana: Pathway Publishers, 1992), 252-265. See the preface and note 1, above.

174. Original: "You have allowed the sun of nature to rise. . . ."

175. See Gen. 28:10-17.

176. See Deut. 6:7; Ps. 1:2.

177. Ps. 121:4-6.

178. "Holy watchers" appear in Dan. 4:13, 17, 23.

179. See 1 Kings 19:5.

180. See Acts 12:6-7.

181. See Matt. 1:20-25; 2:12-13, 19-20, 22.

182. This and the next few sentences are based on Ps. 39:4-9, 12.

183. Based on Heb. 13:14.

184. See Job. 7:2.

185. Based on Ps. 139:16.

186. See Eph. 6:10-17.

187. See 1 Cor. 13:13.

188. See Ps. 42:1-2.

189. See Ps. 84:1.

190. See John 19:1-2, 18, 31-37.

191. Luke 23:43.

192. See Luke 10:30-35.

193. Based on John 11:25.

194. Based on Wisdom of Sol. 3:1, in the Apocrypha.

195. See Rev. 14:13.

196. See Matt. 14:28-31.

197. "Evening time" suggests that this is the prayer of an aged devout person facing death, weary of life's struggles, and eager to flee the sin and evil of the world and to be forever at peace with God. There is a pietistic touch, yet the prayer is not simply individualistic escapism from the physical world. The fourth paragraph shows identification with faithful "ancestors," and the prayer is well grounded in Scripture and the community of faith.

198. For this paragraph and the next one, see Phil. 1:21-23; 1 Cor. 15:50-54; 2 Cor. 5:1-5.

199. Based on John 10:9.

200. See Matt. 22:11-12; Eph. 5:26-27; Rev. 3:20; 7:9; 19:7-8.

201. See Matt. 25:34, 21, 23.

202. Compare Ps. 90.

203. See Heb. 13:14; Ps. 90:12.

204. This prayer reflects a custom of having the major funeral service right after the burial. Such a practice differs from Amish custom but is preserved among the Old Order Mennonites of Ontario. This prayer is one of seven from the 1846 (first) Canadian edition of *Christenpflicht*, printed at Berlin, Upper Canada, by Heinrich Eby, son of the pioneer Mennonite bishop Benjamin Eby (1785-1853). These clues point toward Benjamin Eby as the likely editor and compiler of the 1846 Canadian edition, according to David Luthy, in a letter of

Oct. 16, 1995. See note 2, above.

205. Compare Phil. 2:12; Heb. 12:14; 3:11—4:11.

206. See John 9:4.

207. Original: "unwiedergebornen (unreborn, not born from above)." See note 32, above.

208. See Matt. 25:1-30.

209. Original: "das Eine was uns noth ist." Compare Luther's *Bibel*, Luke 10:42, "Eins aber ist not (only one thing is needed)."

210. See 2 Cor. 5:18-20; Rom. 5:1; Heb. 12:14; 3:11—4:11.

211. See Matt. 22:30; Mark 12:25; Luke 20:36. Here the German version gives the reference for the Lord's Prayer but not the text, supplied and adapted here from KJV to match the quotation on page 21, above.

Index

⚜ome topics are so pervasive that they are not listed below, such as names of God, Christ, and the Holy Spirit; eternity, faith, glory, grace, love, mercy, righteous(ness), thanks, Word, etc. Also see the contents, on pages 5-7, and the notes, on pages 137-146.

✣

Translator and Editor

Leonard Gross, consulting archivist at the Archives of the Mennonite Church, served as executive secretary of the Historical Committee of the Mennonite Church and director of its archives and historical research program during 1970-1990.

Earlier, Gross worked with youth in North Germany on assignment with Mennonite Central Committee. He studied as a Fulbright Scholar at the University of Basel, with doctoral studies in church history, general history, and New Testament.

Gross is the author of *The Golden Years of the Hutterites, 1565-1578*. He translated and edited *Golden Apples in Silver Bowls*, and cooperated to produce *Selected Hutterian Documents in Translation, 1542-1654*.

Leonard is a member of College Mennonite Church, Goshen, Indiana. He is married to Irene Geiser, and they are the parents of two grown daughters, Suzanne and Valerie.